Ruth Bell Graham

CELEBRATING AN EXTRAORDINARY LIFE

D0109204

To my wonderful
friend Rachel,
who has always
been there for me.
Many blessings to
you.
Love,
Karen

Happy Birthday
2014

RUTH *Bell* GRAHAM

CELEBRATING
an EXTRAORDINARY
Life

Compiled by
STEPHEN GRIFFITH

THOMAS NELSON
Since 1798

NASHVILLE DALLAS MEXICO CITY RIO DE JANEIRO BEIJING

© 2003 by Ruth Graham Bell.

All rights reserved. No portion of this book may be reproduced, stored in a retrieval system, or transmitted in any form or by any means—electronic, mechanical, photocopy, recording, or any other—except for brief quotation in printed reviews, without the prior permission of the publisher.

Published in Nashville, Tennessee, by Thomas Nelson. Thomas Nelson is a trademark of Thomas Nelson, Inc.

Thomas Nelson, Inc., titles may be purchased in bulk for educational, business, fund-raising, or sales promotional use. For information, please e-mail SpecialMarkets@ThomasNelson.com.

Unless otherwise marked, Scripture quotations are taken from the King James Version of the Bible (KJV).

Scriptures marked NIV are taken from The Holy Bible, New International Version. Copyright ©1973, 1978, 1984, International Bible Society. Used by permission of Zondervan Bible Publishers.

Library of Congress Cataloging-in-Publication Data

Ruth Bell Graham : celebrating an extraordinary life / compiled by Stephen Griffith.
    p. cm.
Includes bibliographical references (p.   ) and index.
ISBN-10: 0-8499-1763-8 (HC)
ISBN-13: 978-0-8499-1763-9 (HC)
ISBN-10: 0-8499-1986-X (TP)
ISBN-13: 978-0-8499-1986-2 (TP)
    1. Graham, Ruth Bell. 2. Baptists—United States—Biography. 3. Evangelists' spouses—United States—Biography. 4. Spouses of clergy—United States—Biography. 5. Children of missionaries—China—Biography. 6. Graham, Billy, 1918– I. Graham, Ruth Bell. II. Griffith, Stephen.
    BX6495.G666R88 2003
    269'.2'092—dc22   2003014583

Printed in the United States of America
07 08 09 10 BPI 5 4 3 2 1

Contents

SECTION ONE: LIFE'S BUILDING BLOCKS

CHAPTER ONE: HOME

CHAPTER TWO: PARENTS

CHAPTER THREE: CHARACTER

SECTION TWO: BUILDING A LIFE

CHAPTER FOUR: BILLY, PART ONE (COURTING)

CHAPTER FIVE: BILLY, PART TWO (MARRIED LIFE)

CHAPTER SIX: FAMILY

CONTRIBUTORS
(and their relationship to Ruth Bell Graham)

Jim Bakker, former PTL founder and evangelist
Berdjette Tchividjian Barker, oldest granddaughter
Barbara Bush, former first lady and wife of
    President George Walker Bush
Patricia Cornwell, best-selling author
Julie Nixon Eisenhower, daughter of former
    President Richard Nixon
Jean Graham Ford, sister-in-law
Leighton Ford, evangelist and brother-in-law
Gay Currie Fox, childhood friend
Evelyn Freeland, longtime secretary
Betty Frist, neighbor
Billy Graham, evangelist and husband
Franklin Graham, son
Stephen Griffith, writer/editor
Dr. Olson Huff, pediatrician
Claudia (Lady Bird) Johnson, former first lady and
    wife of President Lyndon Johnson
Jan Karon, best-selling author
Anne Graham Lotz, daughter
Andie MacDowell, actress
Ruth Graham McIntyre, daughter
Rosa Bell Montgomery, sister
Kitty Peterson, childhood friend
John Pollock, author
Maurie Scobie, longtime personal assistant
Betty Ruth Barrows Seera, daughter of Cliff and Billie Barrows

George Beverly Shea, singer and original member of the
    Crusade Team
Karlene Shea, former worker at the Montreat office
    and wife of George Beverly Shea
Gigi Graham Tchividjian, daughter
Calvin Thielmann, former pastor
Richard Jesse Watson, author/illustrator

According to *Webster's New World Dictionary*, grace is defined as "beauty or charm of form, composition, movement, or expression." Ruth Bell Graham is the embodiment of grace. She has nothing to prove, no one to compete with, and she's wholly at peace with herself.

—Guy Kawasaki, *Hindsights*

INTRODUCTION

TWO PHOTOS

STEPHEN GRIFFITH

*S*earching through the attic, rifling through a box of photos, one made me catch my breath. Like a prospector finding a golden nugget, I lifted the photo from its cardboard casket. The girl's beauty was striking.

The girl was certainly college age, but there was no description, date, or photographer's credit. The photo was black and white with the formerly white edges turned yellow, the only indication the picture was aged. The girl sat playfully cross-legged on a couch and I could see the hint of her high-laced boots, an interesting choice to go with the cotton gingham dress. The dress was homemade, although the details showed a certain skill in the sewing, trimmed with rickrack, short puffed sleeves with a cuff, and a fitted bodice.

With her pigtails it appeared she was going to a costume ball as Dorothy Gale from Kansas. But I doubted it; she looked too comfortable for it to be a costume. And it was that comfort, that confidence, that kept drawing me back to the photo. How was that self-assurance conveyed? The posture? The expression? And where did that buoyancy come from? Studying her features, I got the sincere impression that the face, radiating with a smile, was lit from within. In that face I read self-confidence, someone at home with who she was. Her eyes and smile were sparked with life and humor, plus a slight hint of mischief.

I put the photo back. It wasn't exactly what I was looking for at the time. But there was no doubt as to the identity of the girl, now in her eighties. The same smile, confidence, and mischievousness grace her face today.

The photo of the young beauty was probably snapped in 1940 or 1941. She looks about twenty years of age, and perhaps the shutter clicked before she married. I like to imagine history at that turning point, poised to go off in other directions.

If the photo was taken in 1940, it would be another forty-seven years before I met Ruth Bell Graham, the girl in the photo, ready to play my bit role in her life. Having known her for only fifteen years, I fully admit that almost everyone interviewed for this book has a fuller and more intimate history with Ruth.

But I do know her heart. I've helped her with her books for those fifteen years and tried to help put her thoughts, prayers, poems, and photos on paper to share with others.

One of the latest projects I worked on was the UNC-TV special *Ruth and Billy Graham: What Grace Provides*, helping producer Donna Campbell with interviews and logistics. As I was listening to the interviews, I noticed one repeated phrase: "Ruth is the most unforgettable character I've ever known."

So the seed for another book was planted. After all, as Patricia Cornwell (best-selling author and Ruth's biographer) has said, "Everyone who knows Ruth knows she is an extremely talented person and that there is so much to Ruth, there is not any biography or film that could capture her fully."

The idea behind this book is to create another photo of Ruth Bell Graham; but instead of looking for a photo in the attic, I rummaged and rifled through countless interviews, articles, and books in an attempt to create a multidimensional picture, in words, of a woman who has quietly influenced many lives and without doubt is the most unforgettable character I've ever known.

ON THE BEAUTY OF RUTH BELL GRAHAM

*I*t is a cliché to say it's her inner beauty, but her inner self and confidence exude to the outer. She's always been beautiful, even from childhood. It's natural. She hasn't focused on it. When you see her out and about you see this beautiful woman, but it's not like she spent an hour making herself perfect. She just *is* beautiful. She puts a little lipstick on and comes out and is gorgeous. I don't think she thinks much about it.

—BERDJETTE TCHIVIDJIAN BARKER

She's beautiful. I was surprised not only by her interior beauty but by her physical beauty. I hope I look like that when I'm eighty. She has this unbelievable skin, elegance, and presence. She's a bright and beautiful woman who had to live behind a strong, powerful man, yet not lose herself.

—ANDIE MACDOWELL

Ruth Graham, with daughter Gigi, novelist Patricia Cornwell, and Andie MacDowell at the press conference for her 80th birthday celebration.

LIFE'S BUILDING BLOCKS

*L*ife is a voyage. The winds of life come strong
From every point; yet each will speed thy course along,
If thou with steady hand when tempests blow
Canst keep thy course aright and never once let go.
—THEODORE CHICKERING WILLIAMS, *The Voyage of Life*

Chapter One

HOME

Mother does think of China as home. When she's coming out of surgery and she's still under the effects of anesthesia, she'll start talking like she's home in China. Those times in China were precious for her.

—GIGI GRAHAM TCHIVIDJIAN

HER HEART'S STILL IN CHINA
ANNE GRAHAM LOTZ

*A*lthough Mother left China at age eighteen to go to Wheaton College and did not return until 1980, she never forgot China or its people—the land and people of her happy childhood. She read, studied, and interviewed those who might afford any clue about her homeland and how the Christian church was faring under intense persecution. She corresponded with a variety of people who shared her interest. China was in her blood. It became a passion that bore fruit—from individual Chinese friends whom she was able to get released from China through her contacts, to being present as my father sat with the leadership of China to explain to them what he believed about Jesus Christ, to eventually seeing her youngest son start a ministry to the Chinese church. She has seen the doors to China open dramatically to the West and particularly to the gospel, which is her life's one passion.

In 1989, my two sisters and I were privileged to accompany our mother back to China to visit her hometown, Huaiyin. As we toured the grounds of what used to be the Love and Mercy Hospital, Chinese officials told us their plans for the new hospital they were building. When it was Mother's chance to reply, she gave the gospel plainly and clearly. She has the heart of an evangelist. Although her gift is often overshadowed by my father's, Mother's gift is exercised effectively on behalf of individuals. At her deepest core is the desire for individuals to know Christ in a personal and intimate way. My father preaches sermons to the masses, reaching thousands; my mother talks to individuals, loving them one by one, showing her concern for them as people. Early in life spreading the gospel became her purpose.

When China was just reopening to the West, my mother spoke in a hospital where there were many staff members that served with her daddy. My mother told them, you can be a medical doctor and care for the physical needs of a person, but you also need to care for their spiritual needs. She gave them the gospel and told them how they could receive Christ by faith. I saw that boldness in her continuing not only what my grandfather had been about but what my father is about and what she's always been about but just not had as many opportunities to verbalize in settings like that. It was remarkable. We went back to see her childhood home and she could remember the streets and the houses. She wanted to see a house where some fellow missionaries were raised, and we found out it was a house church.

Many interesting things happened on that trip. I saw many things about my mother: her love for detail, her love of beauty. The Chinese people have such an eye for beauty.

I could see things around the house at Montreat, the way she arranged flowers, the way she's arranged something, the contrast of colors, that was coming out of what she experienced as a child growing up in China. It helped enrich my understanding of my mother to see the kind of atmosphere where my mother was raised. My grandmother went to China as a bride of six weeks, at a time when China seldom saw westerners. It was a difficult time. To cook or to drink water, my grandmother had to get it from the river and then boil it and pass it through cheesecloth five different times before she could even use it. It was hardship. She bore five children there and buried one. It's the kind of life you read about but hope you never experience.

My mother was raised by people like that: committed, strong, and fun.

RUTH'S CHILDHOOD

*R*uth's childhood was spent in the Chinese village of Tsingkiangpu, where her medical missionary parents had established a three-hundred-and-eighty-bed hospital. From the time she was a baby, Ruth was familiar with death and suffering. . . . Bubonic plague and other diseases were rampant. Death was a very real presence—not only death from disease. They lived in bandit country and every night some three hundred people were captured—some tortured, some killed. "I don't believe I ever went to sleep without hearing the sound of gunshots," she said. During the conflict between the Japanese and Chinese in the late 1930s, Ruth became accustomed to Japanese bombers flying over the house—so low she could see the bombs in the bomb racks. Today her daughter Gigi says, "Mother just doesn't know what it means to be afraid."

—JULIE NIXON EISENHOWER

Ruth, Virginia, Virginia Jr., Rosa, and Dr. Bell waiting to begin their journey to Shanghai.

Ruth said there was hardly a night that passed that they didn't hear gunshots and fighting. But because Dr. and Mrs. Bell were so assured in their hearts that this was where God wanted them to be, they didn't dwell on fear. They felt God was going to protect them. So Ruth learned early on not to be afraid of these things. That goes hand in hand with her incredibly deep faith.

—MAURIE SCOBIE

Ruth's mother told me of one incident that occurred when Ruth was a tiny child in China. Bandits were approaching the missionary compound where they lived, and the shooting was getting closer and closer and louder and louder. Mrs. Bell hurried toward Ruth's room, intent on quelling her fears, and called out, "Ruth, there's nothing to be afraid of." She heard Ruth answer cheerily, "Who's afraid?"

This attitude has been typical of her throughout her life. When she was a little older, she was so devoted to Christ that her all-consuming desire was to be a martyr for him. Every day she'd pray fervently and audibly that God would allow the bandits to capture and behead her.

Her sister, Rosa, hearing her, would pray in concern (and probably a little exasperation): "Lord, don't listen to her."

—BETTY FRIST

THE FORMATIVE YEARS
JOHN POLLOCK

*T*he formative years of Rosa and Ruth in the troubled China of the 1920s, before either had reached the age of ten, were years of security, affection, discipline, and fun.

"I remember our home," said Ruth, "as rather large, gray brick, with a red tin roof and a large porch around two sides of the house. As you came in the front door there was a vestibule, with a table and a mirror on the left and a wooden seat around two sides where visitors could sit and be greeted. To the left was Daddy's study with an old roll-top desk and bookshelves containing his medical books and quite a row of Edgar Wallace detective stories. In the corner was a big, old safe. We kids used to crawl around the floor; sometimes we could find Chinese pennies that had been dropped when the money was deposited. We used to love to go hunting for pennies around the safe.

"To the right of the entrance hall was the living room, and it was blue—blue cushions, curtains, and flowered wallpaper. Mother had some furniture that her father had made, but most of it had been made by the local carpenter. A window seat overlooked the front porch, and two windows were at the far side with an upright piano between. In the center of the room was a table, and there were Chinese rugs on the floor, blue with floral designs around the edge, and a little fireplace in the corner of the room around which we sat on winter evenings. I always remember home as being the most comfortable place in the world."

The living-room fireplace burned coal from Shantung, and the dining room had a coal stove with a tin pipe to heat the room above. Each bedroom had a little tin stove fed by soybean stalks or odds and ends of paper. In winter the children had their weekly bath in a tin tub in front of the little burner upstairs: "The half of you that was away from the trash burner would freeze and the other half would be red-hot!"

The Bells usually ate American-style food. Although they enjoyed Chinese dishes frequently, the home was frankly American for the children's sake. One of the Chinese doctors said to Bell, "We don't mind you having houses larger than ours; we like you to have them. All we want to know is that the door is also open to us." And it was.

After lunch was served, both parents went to work at the hospital. Mrs. Bell had charge of the women's clinic and could be counted on to be out of the way for two hours. The two children then proceeded to scrap. These two little girls who afterward became such devoted sisters "hated each other. We fought all the time. When Mother was out of the way, we really tore into it. We fought verbally and with our hands and feet, and the servants used to line up and bet on who was going to win."

The children may have supposed their parents were in blissful ignorance, but when Rosa was twenty and Ruth eighteen and both in college in America, Nelson Bell remarked to his mother in a letter from China: "Their devotion to each other has been a comfort to us—they used to scrap like cats and dogs. Each is constantly writing something nice about the other."

Every evening the Bell family changed their workday clothes, ate dinner, and then gathered around the fireplace in the living room with its blue motif and fine old French etchings which Virginia had inherited. After dark the risk of kidnapping, gunfire, and banditry kept all citizens off the streets. Although a rare emergency might arrive at the gate escorted by a policeman or soldier, and Nelson occasionally drove to the city or to Hwalan on an urgent call, normally, except for the usual round of the wards after supper, he was free for family fun. They played party games, word games, and popular pastimes now forgotten, such as caroms, Crokinole, and Flinch. But their greatest relaxation was reading aloud. Nelson and Virginia had discovered this special pleasure as early as the winter of 1918, starting with Dickens and Scott. For Rosa and Ruth they began with favorites such as *Little Lord Fauntleroy*, as they grew, the girls enjoyed *David Copperfield, A Tale of Two Cities, Ivanhoe,* Kingsley's *Hypatta,* and many other classics. Sometimes it would be just "a frivolous tale." Virginia read aloud to the children at other times of the day when they were small; in the evenings Nelson read the larger share while his wife and daughters sewed or knitted.

About the nights, Ruth said, "I can never recall going to sleep at night without hearing gunshots in the countryside around the house." If warlords or bandits were quiet, it was a neighbors' quarrel or robbery or even an accident. "I remember one tremendous fire in the city. We went up to the third-floor attic window where we could see it and hear the explosions. We thought the city was being invaded. The whole skyline was lit up. Later we learned that some barges containing five-gallon tins of oil had caught on fire and the oil tins were exploding. . . . I think the greatest tribute to Mother's courage is that we children never sensed fear and we ourselves never had any fear. This is bound to reflect your parents. If they had been nervous, we would have been nervous."

(adapted from *A Foreign Devil in China*)

GROWING UP IN CHINA
ROSA BELL MONTGOMERY

*M*other and Daddy sheltered us from as much as they could, but what they couldn't, they were just matter-of-fact about. So we didn't dwell on those things. For instance, Ruth once found a baby on the streets that had been thrown out by her parents. She quickly realized the child was not dead although there were flies crawling over the poor little naked thing. She went back to get help but unfortunately the baby later died. These were the type of things we saw all the time as children. But there were also so many joyous occasions and happy times that things balanced out.

I remember one Sunday afternoon Mother and Daddy were sitting on the side porch because that was the shady side at that time of the day. Sunday was a day we had to behave ourselves. Mother and Daddy never took anything from us that they didn't supply us

Nelson Bell, Ruth, Rosa, and Virginia Bell.

with something better. Sunday was a day that was set apart differ-ent from the rest of the week. So on Sunday we didn't sing secular songs, we didn't read secular books, and we didn't play secular games. And we were supposed to be quieter than our activities on other days. But Sundays were full of things we could do. Mother saved all the Sunday school papers we could read on Sunday. We played Bible games on Sunday. We learned to sing harmony around the piano. It was a really happy day. We never dreaded Sunday.

This particular afternoon they were sitting quietly enjoying each other's company. Ruth and I were supposedly playing nicely out in the yard. Ruth had a creepy-crawly bug of some kind. One glance at it and that was enough for me. I don't remember what it looked like except it was awful. Well, she started to chase me with it. I screeched and hollered and the more I screeched and hollered, the happier I was. We went round and round the yard until Daddy said, "Rosa, come here right now." He set me down to behave myself. It was all Ruth's fault, and she didn't get bawled out.

Those kinds of things were irritating. But I could be just as irri-tating back to her.

In the early days, we were antagonists. When Mother and Daddy were at the clinic in the afternoon we would get into it. The ser-vants would stand around and place bets on who was going to win. So they just egged us on.

The older we got the better friends we became. Even with our fighting it was just with each other. Let someone outside be criti-cal and we were instantly at the other's defense. So we were con-stantly looking out for each other as sisters; as friends we were antagonists. One of the nicest things she did for me was while we were in college. It was Christmastime and we were going to stay on campus for the holidays. I can't remember why, but I was sad and Ruth knew I was sad. She went out and bought a little tree, before they made artificial trees, and made ornaments. She cut out a picture from a Christmas card, a star from silver paper, and a whole bunch of little things like that and strung them on the tree and presented it to me. What a sweet thing for her to do, and I even appreciated it back in those days. It was such a loving thing. And she was always doing loving things. I can't fault her on that for one minute.

PARENTAL DISCIPLINE
JOHN POLLOCK

*I*f the Bell children were naughty, they were spanked or switched, whichever was appropriate. "Punishments were generously dished out, but we knew they loved us." They— and the two younger children later—were disciplined without being repressed. With two adoring parents who always "seemed very young," who never punished in anger or selfishness, the children did not feel nagged or scolded. Rosa and Ruth regard the strictness as one reason why they recollect childhood with such happiness.

Defiance or disobedience met inevitable doom. Elbows on the lunch table were swept off in a trice. Virginia was chief disciplinarian, but Ruth joked, "It seems to me they ganged up on us."

"We could not divide and conquer them," added Rosa. "If we asked Daddy for permission to do something and he said 'No,' we might go to Mother and say, 'Mother, may we do thus and so?' And

Dr. Bell performing surgery at the Love and Mercy Hospital.

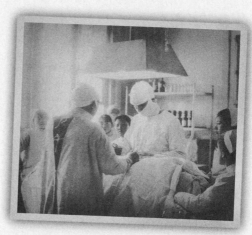

instead of saying 'Yes,' she would say, 'What did your father say?' 'He said no.' 'Then why did you come and ask me?' Then we'd do Daddy the same way. We'd ask Mother, 'May we do thus and so?' And if she'd say, 'Absolutely not,' we'd go and say, 'Daddy, may we do thus and so?' 'What does your mother say?' 'Well, she said we couldn't.' 'Then why did you ask me?'

"But if it was something that we really and truly wanted to do very badly, and Mother had said no and we couldn't approach her any further on the subject, we'd say, 'Daddy, this is something that is very important and won't you reconsider?' He would give it his attention. And if he felt that it was all right, he would check with Mother first. They would hash it out together without us eavesdropping. If there was a good, substantial reason why we couldn't be indulged, the answer would continue to be no. But if it was reasonable that we should have our way, they would say, 'We have discussed it and have decided you may do it.'"

(adapted from A Foreign Devil in China)

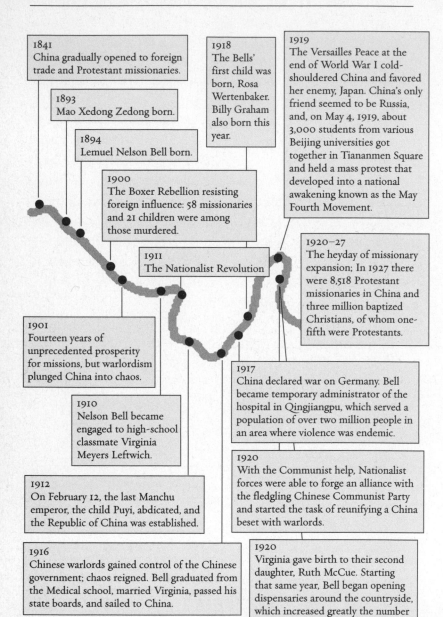

1841
China gradually opened to foreign trade and Protestant missionaries.

1893
Mao Xedong Zedong born.

1894
Lemuel Nelson Bell born.

1900
The Boxer Rebellion resisting foreign influence: 58 missionaries and 21 children were among those murdered.

1911
The Nationalist Revolution

1901
Fourteen years of unprecedented prosperity for missions, but warlordism plunged China into chaos.

1910
Nelson Bell became engaged to high-school classmate Virginia Meyers Leftwich.

1912
On February 12, the last Manchu emperor, the child Puyi, abdicated, and the Republic of China was established.

1916
Chinese warlords gained control of the Chinese government; chaos reigned. Bell graduated from the Medical school, married Virginia, passed his state boards, and sailed to China.

1918
The Bells' first child was born, Rosa Wertenbaker. Billy Graham also born this year.

1919
The Versailles Peace at the end of World War I cold-shouldered China and favored her enemy, Japan. China's only friend seemed to be Russia and, on May 4, 1919, about 3,000 students from various Beijing universities got together in Tiananmen Square and held a mass protest that developed into a national awakening known as the May Fourth Movement.

1920–27
The heyday of missionary expansion; In 1927 there were 8,518 Protestant missionaries in China and three million baptized Christians, of whom one-fifth were Protestants.

1917
China declared war on Germany. Bell became temporary administrator of the hospital in Qingjiangpu, which served a population of over two million people in an area where violence was endemic.

1920
With the Communist help, Nationalist forces were able to forge an alliance with the fledgling Chinese Communist Party and started the task of reunifying a China beset with warlords.

1920
Virginia gave birth to their second daughter, Ruth McCue. Starting that same year, Bell began opening dispensaries around the countryside, which increased greatly the number they were able to serve.

1921
The Nationalists ruled over southern China but turned to the new Communist government of the Soviet Union for help. The missionaries at Qingjiangpu briefly evacuated because of threatened violence from large gangs in the area.

1932
Between 1924 and 1934, twenty-nine Protestant missionaries were killed and a number kidnapped. To survive, the church had to achieve genuine autonomy. A nationwide spiritual awakening in the 1930s facilitated this development, but continuing civil war boded ill for the future.

1932
The Bell children were educated at home by Virginia until 1932. In that year Rosa was sent to a Christian school for western children in Pyengyang, Korea.

1931
Mao Zedong proclaimed the establishment of the Chinese Soviet Republic under his chairmanship.

1925
During the summer the Nationalist government set out on the long-delayed Northern Expedition against the northern warlords. Within nine months, half of China had been conquered.

1927
Civil war continued. There now were three capitals in China: the internationally recognized warlord regime in Beijing; the Communist and left-wing Guomindang regime at Wuhan; and the right-wing civilian-military regime at Nanjing, which would remain the Nationalist capital for the next decade.

1925
The Bells' first son, Nelson Jr., was born, but in October of the same year the baby died of amoebic dysentery.

1926
The Nationalist movement divided into left- and right-wing factions, and the Communist bloc within it was also growing but continued fighting against the warlords. Nearly all 8,000 Protestant missionaries fled during chaos of the Northern Expedition. The rapid growth of the Communist movement was now a serious threat. Nelson Bell became the superintendent of the hospital at Qingjiangpu.

1928
Missionaries evacuated the city to avoid advancing Nationalist armies. The Bells went to Shanghai and then returned to the United States on furlough. They stayed until the birth of their daughter, Virginia, and returned to China at the end of the year. All of China was at least nominally under Nationalist control, and the Nanjing government received prompt international recognition as the sole legitimate government of China.

1935
The family Bells returned to the United States on furlough in 1935 and lived in Montreat, North Carolina, where the girls went to school.

1934
Ruth followed Rosa to Pyengyang, Korea. In December 1934 another child, Benjamin Clayton, was added to the family. Billy Graham experienced a religious conversion that shaped the direction of his life.

1936
In August, all the Bells returned to China except for Rosa, who enrolled at Wheaton College as a freshman.

1937
Japan mounted a full-scale attack against China. Once whole-scale war had been launched, it didn't take the Japanese long to occupy the major coastal cities and commit atrocities. By the time the war had ended in 1945, 20 million Chinese had died at the hands of the Japanese. The war with Japan (1937-45) severely tested the Chinese Church and left China at the mercy of Communism. Though 3,000 missionaries again dispersed throughout the country, their time was short. At the insistence of the American government, the missionaries evacuated Qingjiangpu in 1937 to avoid advancing Japanese troops.

1934
Mao Zedong led the Long March (1934-35) to Shaanxi, where the Communists established their base. The Communists would grow rapidly for the next ten years. Contributing to this growth would be a combination of internal and external circumstances. Conflict with Japan, which would continue from the 1930s to the end of World War II, was the other force (besides the Communists themselves) that would undermine the Nationalist government. December 1934, missionaries John and Betty Stam were murdered by Communist troops.

1939
When the Qingjiangpu was occupied by the Japanese in February, Nelson Bell was able to persuade them to allow the missionaries to continue their work. In April of the same year, the family returned to the United States for a brief furlough. They returned to China in September.

1941
In May, the Bell family returned to the United States. They settled in Montreat. During the summer, Billy Graham, a classmate of Ruth's, came to Montreat to meet the family.

1937
In October, Ruth sailed back to the United States to enroll in Wheaton College.

1941-1946
Most missionaries interred or evacuated but returned to China after WWII.

1943
Billy Graham and Ruth Bell married.

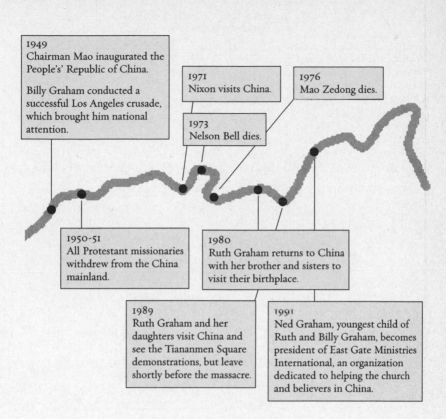

1949
Chairman Mao inaugurated the People's' Republic of China.

Billy Graham conducted a successful Los Angeles crusade, which brought him national attention.

1971
Nixon visits China.

1976
Mao Zedong dies.

1973
Nelson Bell dies.

1950-51
All Protestant missionaries withdrew from the China mainland.

1980
Ruth Graham returns to China with her brother and sisters to visit their birthplace.

1989
Ruth Graham and her daughters visit China and see the Tiananmen Square demonstrations, but leave shortly before the massacre.

1991
Ned Graham, youngest child of Ruth and Billy Graham, becomes president of East Gate Ministries International, an organization dedicated to helping the church and believers in China.

Chapter Two

PARENTS

Judicious mothers will always keep in mind that they are the first book read, and the last put aside, in every child's library.

—C. LENOX REMOND

MOTHER'S ROLE MODELS
RUTH GRAHAM MCINTYRE

Mother was born in China during the time of warlords and bandits. She grew up hearing gunfire in the distance at night. Then the Japanese invaded China. She can recall seeing the bombs in their berths as the planes swooped low over their compound. But she doesn't remember fear being part of her childhood. She lost a brother to dysentery when he was eighteen months old but remembers no lingering shadow of sorrow. Her mother frequently suffered debilitating migraine headaches and would have to go to bed in a darkened room. Yet my mother's overwhelming memory was the effort her own mother made to keep their home running smoothly and to create a happy environment for the family.

Her mother, Virginia Bell, was very talented and creative in her homemaking skills. She was a single-mindedly supportive wife for Nelson Bell. After they left China to return to the States, he set up a private medical practice in Asheville, North Carolina. When he was called to an emergency in the night, she, too, would get up, ride the thirty minutes to the hospital, and wait in the car until he was through, just to keep him company. Her philosophy of child rearing was simple: Her job was not to make her children happy but to make them good. She succeeded in doing both well. Her life's commitment was to serve Jesus Christ, her husband, and her family.

My mother's father, Nelson Bell, was a busy surgeon who became chief of staff of one of the world's largest Presbyterian hospitals in China at the time. He created a secure, loving home filled with music, quality family experience, and humor. In turn, he adored his wife, who had been his childhood sweetheart. His fidelity to Christ and His service never wavered. His perspective was to serve the whole person, not just see a person "saved." At times in China, he would give his own blood to save a patient. But he knew eventually all his patients would die and he was very concerned with the condition of their souls. He was staunch in his belief in the Bible as the infallible Word of God. In spite of his responsibilities and schedule, he was never too busy for interruptions or impromptu visits with those who came to his back door. He made weekly visits to comfort those confined in the hospital. He was always a friend.

As Mother's role models, her parents exercised a profound effect upon the development of her character and laid the foundations for who she is. I observe traits in her now that I know were formed long ago by these two godly people who were firmly dedicated to Christ and committed to their family.

MOTHER AND DADDY
ROSA BELL MONTGOMERY

*O*ur parents were always so caring, so encouraging, and so pleased with any accomplishment. The first picture [my sister] Ruth ever drew was of Mickey Mouse. They praised that thing like it was a Rembrandt. "Look at that. Our daughter drew that." They were always telling people, "Our daughters are so great and so wonderful."

Mother was always a very helpful person. She was always supportive of Daddy, but she was her own person. He never discouraged her. He found out early in their marriage that some of her ideas were a lot better than his. So, in those particular categories like making a home and decorating, he let her lead the way. Then it got so that she was also an excellent diagnostician. She worked in the woman's clinic with him every afternoon. And sometimes she would say, "Nelson, this is what's wrong with this patient," and she would turn out to be right every time. She was an extremely practical person. When I was a junior in college I took an ethics class, and when I was home for the summer, I asked my mother to take the final exam, which I had kept. I was humiliated; she did better than I did. But it spelled to my mind that ethics was actually the application of common sense. And my mother had a huge dose of common sense.

If Mother had fears, she didn't express them to us. Mother and Daddy were very matter-of-fact when it came to the soldiers and bandits in China. I remember one time when I spent the whole afternoon on the roof of our house so I could see over the compound wall watching people coming from the country villages to the city, because the people were leaving the villages to get out of the way of the communists coming down out of the north. We weren't at all concerned because Mother wasn't concerned, but that night we found out she had packed our things and the next day we were sent about ten miles away to protect us from possible trouble. Mother wanted us to be safe, but she wasn't about to leave my dad. Her theme was, "Whither thou goest, I will go." She would never leave Daddy's side.

NELSON BELL
JOHN POLLOCK

*W*hen Nelson Bell received his medical degree on June 6, 1916, he was only twenty-one years old. To qualify so young was rare. On June 30, 1916, Nelson and Virginia were married in the First Presbyterian Church, Waynesboro, Virginia, and a few weeks later, Nelson passed his state board examinations. By December 4th of that year, after a stormy passage of nineteen days from Seattle, the Bells had landed at the International Settlement in Shanghai. Then, at the end of October 1917 the main physician, Dr. Woods, in Tsingkiangpu, left on his overdue furlough, not to be back until 1919. Thus at the age of twenty-three, after being qualified a mere seventeen months, Nelson Bell became superintendent of the only hospital in an area where more than two million people lived.

Such was the intensity of Nelson Bell's life, and the challenge of China was enormous.

Sufferers often came to the hospital only as a last resort, held back by prejudice against the "foreign devil." Though the phrase was seldom used to a foreigner's face, except by children, the country people assumed that "outer barbarians" were ignorant and sinister. Yet the Chinese folk doctors offered no effective relief apart from a few herbal remedies or ancient drugs.

Tropical diseases were common, especially those which are aggravated by malnutrition, drought, or floods. Even in a good year peasants and laborers subsisted on an inadequate diet.

But it was gunshot or other wounds that often took as many as 50 of the 170 beds at once. Men and women were shot or knifed in family or neighborhood quarrels. Bandits blindfolded their kidnapped victims by splashing warm pitch on their eyes. Soon the distraught relatives received a small parcel. Inside was a finger or toe and a ransom demand. If they delayed, a larger packet would be sent containing something even more horrific. After ransom the victim would be taken to the hospital for repair. Often the bandits broke into farmhouses, stripped and tied up their owners, and burned them until they revealed the hiding place of their money. Other inhumanities could sicken even a doctor used to broken bodies. "I feel sometimes like I am looking down into the very mouth of hell itself," Dr. Woods had said.

But Nelson Bell approached these problems with unflinching commitment and zest. Few other doctors possessed a sense of humor like Nelson's.

Dr. Bell was a blithe and happy spirit. The Book of Proverbs says, "A merry heart doeth good like a medicine." As Dr. Bell went through the wards on his rounds, he would have fun and laughter for everybody—a bit of personal banter here and a joke there. They would all roar at his jokes and loved to see him come and hated to see him go.

Without a sense of humor, a doctor in China at that time might well be driven to nervous breakdown by the delays, aggravations, broken promises, and a hundred and one pinpricks. Nelson's humor not only bubbled over but frequently relieved tensions.

And with his growing family he would also share his sense of humor. For example:

When Nelson came home to lunch, having performed more operations in a morning than a surgeon in America would do in a day, he would start describing the operations to the children in all their gory detail.

"Nelson! Not at the table!" Virginia would command.

"Oh, Mother, let him," the children would cry; they loved every minute.

One day Nelson brought back a tray of glass eyes, which had just arrived. For fun he inserted one over his own eye, giving a most gruesome effect.

Bell also possessed a need for speed.

To help him get around, friends at home clubbed together to give him a Harley-Davidson motorcycle with sidecar. Nelson's prowess with the motorcycle became legendary at Tsingkiangpu, and he became a familiar sight sputtering across the canal bridge on a call to the inner city.

Nelson tended to be a little frisky with that motorcycle. Once in a daredevil spirit he rode up the steep incline of the high outer mud wall of the city with Ed Currie, another missionary, in the sidecar. Just before the top the engine stalled and the heavy machine turned turtle on Nelson, who by all the laws of gravity should have been crushed to death. He landed in a slight depression and emerged unscathed.

Another quality he possessed was a determination when he was convinced of the soundness of an idea.

When Dr. James Woods returned to Tsingkiangpu, the two strong-willed men often had some frank exchanges, but Woods and Bell remained the firmest of friends, never letting arguments grow into grudges. G. K. Chesterton once said, "People quarrel because they cannot argue." Woods and Bell knew how to argue.

Perhaps some of the characteristics people love about Ruth were easy to come by—heredity.

(adapted from *A Foreign Devil in China*)

MOTHER AND GRANDFATHER'S IMPACT ON DADDY'S WORLD VIEW

I think my mother impacted my father's world view enormously—not just my mother, but also my mother's father, Nelson Bell. Before he died, I would say he was my father's closest friend, his closest confidant, and it was an enormous loss. I can even remember back when my grandfather died; I remember that sense of loss. Nobody has ever replaced that position in my father's life. And my grandfather helped counsel him and guide him in so many of his views and the way he set up his organization and the way he handled his own ministry. Such integrity—a lot of that was emphasized by my grandfather. At the very beginning, he helped my father make decisions that have borne fruit, even now. My father had a heart for the world, but my mother and grandfather brought it into focus.

—ANNE GRAHAM LOTZ

Mother was born and raised in China and went to school in North Korea. She knew the world in a way my father didn't. My mother and father agreed together that they should take the opportunities overseas when they came. I think she was a help.

—FRANKLIN GRAHAM

Virginia Bell
John Pollock

t the end of October 1917, Nelson took over for Dr. Woods at the hospital in Tsingkiangpu, China. Virginia was expecting her first baby, but she also took the place of Mrs. Woods in running the hospital's housekeeping department and helping in the dispensary and at operations. Less than three years later, Virginia was [expecting] her second baby, and on June 10, 1920, Ruth Bell was born.

Nelson once wrote: "We live surrounded by serious contagious diseases and are simply in God's hands. Unless it is His will that we should be taken ill, nothing can harm us." Virginia could say the same, but she had a daily fight against dirt and germs, especially the prevalent trachoma. Any lapse might lead to illness.

This battle against germs, amid the tensions of civil disturbance and the pressure of her hospital work, imposed a heavy strain on Virginia. Yet severe migraine headaches were the sole nervous reaction. She never complained. She found, however, that the headaches could make her a little short or spicy. And Nelson would be extra considerate and relieve any tension with his marvelous humor. "He could make a joke out of any situation and have everybody laughing. They were a wonderful balance for each other," their children recalled.

While Nelson worked at the hospital, Virginia spent the morning teaching the two girls. The Southern Presbyterians preferred to teach their children on the stations rather than send them away to a school in another part of China; "raising new missionaries" was part of the vocation, a policy which paid off, as many of the children returned to the field as missionaries or in other forms of service.

Virginia proved a born primary teacher, obtained the best books from America, and taught all her children up to the sixth grade; after that they had a tutor until high school. And since all the missionary homes had accumulated good libraries for every age group, the children became great readers.

Virginia taught them music and handwork: embroidery, knitting, crocheting, and sewing. Rosa learned to play the piano, while Ruth enjoyed painting and was interested in art. Their mother was an accomplished needlewoman and dressmaker who passed the skills to her daughters along with a delight in being well dressed. As Ruth has often told interviewers, "My mother didn't see why we should look like the scrapings from the missionary barrel."

For relaxation, in late afternoon Virginia gardened. She had a green thumb, and after a few years her garden or yard was full of shrubs, flowers, and fruit: cherries and strawberries in May; apricots and peaches in June; plums, grapes, and mulberries later. The porch had plants, which were brought into the living room when the chilly weather began.

Again, the fruit doesn't fall too far from the tree.

(adapted from *A Foreign Devil in China*)

AFTER NELSON BELL'S DEATH
EVELYN FREELAND

Ruth's father died suddenly, like Ruth's brother, Clayton. Nelson had been Virginia's caregiver because she could only get around in a wheelchair. But the morning Nelson died, Virginia somehow got out of bed and got to him.

After Ruth's father died, she thought it would be nice for her mother to be up at the house. So she moved her up there but that didn't last very long. Mrs. Bell wanted to be in her own home. She had her friends she played Rook with. They finally moved her back down. Ruth was in and out, bringing meals to her mother all the time and looking after her, doing what she could.

UPON THE DEATH OF VIRGINIA

Ruth began the poem below when she was nineteen years old on Mothers Day, 1940. She finished it thirty-four years later on November 8, 1974, the day her mother died.

As the portrait is unconscious
of the Master Artist's touch,
unaware of growing beauty,
unaware of changing much,
so you have not guessed His working
in your life throughout each year,
have not seen the growing beauty
have not sensed it, Mother dear.
We have seen and marveled greatly
at the Master Artist's skill,
marveled at the lovely picture
daily growing lovelier still;
watched His brush strokes
change each feature
to a likeness of His face,
till in you we see the Master,
feel His presence, glimpse His grace;
pray the fragrance of His presence
may through you seem doubly sweet,
till your years on earth are ended
and the portrait is complete.
—RUTH BELL GRAHAM

Chapter Three

CHARACTER

I look at her and I think, *How can a person become that way?* I don't think her life reflects her faith; I think her life *is* her faith. The way she thinks, the way she talks, and the way she encourages is based on her faith. The Bible is truly her favorite book. How do you become that way? She was forced to make Jesus her best friend for a lot of reasons: because she was alone a lot, because she had to be private. I'm sure that desire grew and it just became natural to her. I like it when you bring up spiritual things. Her face lights up; she loves talking about it.

—BERDJETTE TCHIVIDJIAN BARKER

RUTH'S QUIET ASSURANCE
JULIE NIXON EISENHOWER

*H*er Bible is so worn and soft that Ruth Graham can roll it like a magazine. She turns each page gently so it will not tear. And each page is familiar. She has read and reread it in moments of happiness, moments of pain, when she was seeking answers, and when she was merely expectant. The hundreds of underlined verses and the margins filled with tightly written notations, some in pencil, some in blue or black ink, attest to the extraordinary way in which Ruth Graham communicates with God.

The first time I saw Ruth's Bible was just before Christmas in 1973. The Grahams had spent Saturday night at the White House as guests of my parents, and on Sunday Billy Graham preached at the interdenominational church service in the East Room. After dinner on Saturday, I had asked Ruth if we could visit together before church the next morning.

Ruth Graham had always fascinated me. Her husband is a famous evangelist who has delivered the message of God to millions of people, yet Ruth seems most comfortable when sharing her faith in God quietly, face to face with another seeker. She is spiritual, but at the same time spirited and very much a part of this world. How many other grandmothers take up hang gliding in their fifties? Ruth did. And the first time she jumped off Maggie Valley Mountain she had barely recovered from injuries caused by falling out of a tree when she was putting up a swing for her grandchildren—injuries so severe that it was a week before she regained consciousness. And how many grandmothers borrow their son's black leather jacket and go vrooming along mountain roads on a Harley-Davidson? A daring driver, Ruth (and her motorcycle) ended up in a ditch once, in a lake another time.

The Grahams had been friends of my parents for over twenty years, and though I had talked to Ruth many times before, we had never discussed her faith. This time was different. I was very much aware of the quiet assurance she found in God. I envied it. I wanted to know how Ruth, a woman with spunk and a strong will, could yield her life so completely to God. What gave her the faith to pray about the small things in her life and the large? To pray and to believe that God listens? That God answers?

The third floor of the White House was very quiet that Sunday morning. The domestic staff was busy downstairs preparing the coffee and pastries that would be served after Dr. Graham's sermon. Ruth and I talked in the little sitting room next to their bedroom. It was dark and gloomy despite the bright December sunshine outside. The balustrade that circles the White House roof blocked the sun, and because of its columns the rays that did penetrate the room fell like bars across the furniture and rug. But Ruth seemed radiant, despite the dark room and the fact that she and Billy had stayed up late the night before talking with my mother and father. She laughed as she unbuckled the strap that held her Bible together and excused the worn appearance of the book. The thin black strap looked like a belt and Ruth said that was exactly what it was, a woman's belt that she had cut down for this very purpose. Her hands startled me as she fingered the pages of her Bible. [Her hands] were extremely lined and rough. The only touch of elegance was the wide gold wedding band. But Ruth's hands were capable, surely strong enough to guide a motorcycle or hang, high over the valley, onto her gliding kite.

My questions came rapidly, all at once:

"How do you study the Bible?"

"How do you learn from it?"

"Why all the seeming inconsistencies? Why so many instances of cruelty?"

"Why do you believe in it so deeply?"

Ruth listened quietly until I paused. Then with a smile she said, "I'll try the scatter-gun approach." She held the book in her lap and slowly turned the pages until she came to passages which had meaning for her. I was surprised by her casual, random search, this thumbing through pages, but Ruth explained, "God doesn't deal with people in a formulated way. We shouldn't either." And this was a message she reinforced several times. As I listened, I realized that she offered no easy answers. There were no three steps to comfort or a formula for faith in Ruth Graham's approach. There was nothing pat about her response to my questions.

"It's surprising that there aren't more inconsistencies in the Bible," Ruth said as she leafed through the pages. "So many different people wrote it. And from so many different points of view. It's the differences that make it valid. You know the old story about the four blind men and the elephant. One man held the tail and told his companions that it was a rope. Another ran his hands over the body of the elephant and insisted that it was a wall. The third put his arms around the elephant's leg and said it was a tree trunk. The fourth touched the elephant's trunk and believed it was a snake.

"But in the Bible, none of these differences between the people who wrote it affect the great doctrines."

She turned to the back of her Bible and stopped at chapter eight of Romans. She read out loud to me, "Who shall separate us from the love of Christ? Shall tribulation, or distress, or persecution, or famine, or nakedness, or peril, or sword?" She paused for a moment and then said quietly, "Only sin, sin which touches every man and woman, separates us from God's love." Then she turned to an earlier verse in Romans and read, "For all have sinned, and come short of the glory of God."

As she spoke those words, Ruth was already eagerly turning back to Isaiah. She read the fifth verse of the Fifty-third Chapter, substituting her own name: "But he was wounded for Ruth's transgressions, he was bruised for Ruth's iniquities: the chastisement of Ruth's peace was upon him; and with his stripes, Ruth is healed." She read the words with emotion, her voice almost caressing each syllable, in a Southern accent so marked that it was almost unbelievable that Ruth, the daughter of missionary parents, spoke Chinese before she learned English. She wanted me to know and be assured of the gift of God's love.

"But let's look at the Psalms," Ruth said. "I always draw great help and comfort from them." As she turned page after page, it seemed as if every other verse were underlined. It was apparent that each of them had spoken to her in a special way. When she reached the Thirty-seventh Psalm, Ruth laughed softly. "I've set up camp in Psalm Thirty-seven." She ran her finger down the page and stopped at the fourth verse. "This is the one I think I love more than all others," and she read, "Delight thyself also in the Lord; and he shall give thee the desires of thine heart."

"My favorite translation is from the Septuagint Bible," she said. "It goes—'Indulge thyself also in the Lord.' I love that thought of indulging myself in the Lord. Really, the main thing in studying the Bible," she said, "is to get into it and enjoy it."

At ten-thirty, when Ruth and I had to stop to get ready for the service, I left her with two strong impressions after our hour and a half together. She was not at all a brittle, upbeat Christian who denied all doubts or questions. And she undeniably enjoyed great inner peace. She had not answered all my questions, but somehow that seemed less important now. I was eager to know more about the Bible, and about Ruth herself.

(from *Special People*)

FAMILY PRAYERS AT THE BELL HOUSE

JOHN POLLOCK

*E*ach day in the Bell household began with family prayers. Like any children, Rosa and Ruth occasionally found these irksome or wanted to stay in bed longer. Whoever was not down by the end of the first verse of the hymn had no sugar on her porridge. But both girls noted, with the unfailing perception of childhood, that their father positively enjoyed these daily prayers; they came to realize the importance of his own devotional hour and their mother's devotional time after finishing her household duties.

Rosa spoke for both girls when she said: "I cannot thank God enough for the early training I had in Bible study, that I had parents who believed the Word and who believed in drilling it into their children. We did have to learn a lot of Bible verses, but Mother tried to make it just as interesting and as much fun as possible. They did not make it a punishment—ever. We never had to learn Bible verses because we had been naughty."

(adapted from *A Foreign Devil in China*)

HABITS OF A LIFETIME

I cannot remember when I didn't love the Lord. My earliest recollections are of deepest gratitude to God for having loved me so much that He was willing to send His Son to die in my place.

—RUTH BELL GRAHAM

My mother . . . made God's Word "more to be desired than gold" by her own example. Her loving encouragement, sensitive insights, and unwavering support [have] kept me going during dark moments of weary discouragement.

—ANNE GRAHAM LOTZ

She's got one of the most marked-up Bibles I have ever seen. In the past few years, Mr. Graham has been concerned that she might leave it somewhere or something would happen to it.

—MAURIE SCOBIE

I'm so grateful for her prayers. Prayer is such an intangible thing. I'm not even really sure what it means. But somehow her life embodies prayer. And her prayers are really powerful. The first thing I did when I signed the contract to illustrate Ruth's book *One*

Wintry Night was to make sure I could get a feel for the Middle East, so the publisher provided me with the funds to travel there. Ruth said, "That's great, but take your whole family." I replied, "I can't do that. I can't afford it." She said, "Well, I'll pray you get the money." I had to buy tickets within two weeks and before the two weeks were up, I got the two highest-paying jobs I ever received. I thought, *Wow, who am I dealing with here?*

This has been repeated time and again.

Another time we had a forest fire where I lived and we had to evacuate the art for *One Wintry Night* because the fire was getting dangerously close to our cabin. Fortunately, our house was spared, but fifteen of our neighbors' houses were toast. I just felt this amazing protection and encouragement while I was working on the book.

—RICHARD JESSE WATSON

No matter how enormous the request, for Ruth Graham prayer is "like talking to your best friend," a friend who is by her side twenty-four hours a day. When I had asked Bunny who her mother's best friend was, she seemed puzzled for a moment. She mentioned several people and then said, "I'm not even sure you can say Mother has a best friend, because she doesn't confide in friends that much. Really, the Lord is her best friend." Then Bunny added, as if she felt she had to explain, "I know that is unusual, because most of us—and that includes me—feel we need a human set of ears we can cry or complain to. Even though the Bible teaches us to trust God and to lean on Him." Ruth never gets very far away from God.

—JULIE NIXON EISENHOWER

A Lifetime of Goodbyes

*M*other's loneliness goes back to when she left China to go to school in North Korea. She'd felt so secure in her home in China with her parents; then suddenly [she was] to go off to high school. She's always said that God had been preparing her. It was her boot camp for a "lifetime of goodbyes."

—Gigi Graham Tchividjian

Virginia, Rosa, Ruth, and Virginia on the ship to the Pyeng Yang Foreign School.

A Lifetime of Goodbyes
Gigi Graham Tchividjian

The thirteen-year-old girl lay in the stifling heat of the old missionary home at Number Four Quinsan Gardens in the large port city of Shanghai, China, praying earnestly that she would die before morning.

Dawn broke over the gray city, and obviously God had not seen fit to answer her prayer.

It was September 2, 1933, and time for her to start high school. Her parents had chosen the Pyeng Yang Foreign School in what is today Pyongyang, North Korea.

Her older sister, Rosa, had been there the preceding year, and being a good adjuster, she enjoyed it thoroughly.

But Ruth was different. She was leaving all that she loved and all that was familiar: her home, her parents, her friends, and thirteen years of treasured memories.

Pyeng Yang Foreign School.

Five missionary children boarded the *Nagasake Mane*, berthed in the Whangpoo River, and moved slowly through the muddy waters to where the even muddier waters of the mighty Yangtze River emptied into the East China Sea.

The journey took the better part of a week. Finally they arrived in Pyeng Yang. They were met, transported, and deposited at the school. Ruth found herself in front of the gray-brick girls' dormitory.

The homesickness settled in unmercifully. The days she could somehow manage. It was the nights that became unbearable. Burying her head in her pillow, she tried not to disturb her sleeping roommates.

Night after night, week after week, she cried herself to sleep, silently, miserably.

A few weeks later, Ruth became sick and was sent to the infirmary for several days. She propped herself up on her pillows and spent the entire time reading the Psalms, all 150 of them. The tiny corner room in the infirmary building still holds warm memories for Ruth because of the strength she received from those timeless, timely passages. How could she know that this was her training period? . . . It was her boot camp for a "lifetime of goodbyes."

(from *Footprints of a Pilgrim*)

BUILDING A LIFE

With aching hands and bleeding feet
We dig and heap, lay stone on stone;
We bear the burden and the heat
Of the long day, and wish 'twere done.
Not til the hours of light return,
All we have built do we discern.

—MATTHEW ARNOLD, *Morality*

Chapter Four

BILLY, PART ONE (COURTING)

All the men wanted to date Ruth. She was beautiful and popular. Ruth had a lot of boyfriends. At Wheaton College, her sister Rosa kept count of the different men that she dated. She had a list of fifty-two. I don't think I dated more than two girls at college.

—BILLY GRAHAM

The Belle of Wheaton
Billy Graham

*I*n more ways than one, she was one of the belles of Wheaton campus. I learned this during my first term at Wheaton College from Johnny Streater. To pay his way through college, Johnny ran his own trucking service. For a price, he would haul anything in his little yellow pickup. I gladly accepted his offer of work at fifty cents an hour and spent many afternoons at hard labor, moving furniture and other items around the western Chicago suburbs.

Johnny was a little older than I and had been in the Navy before coming to Wheaton. He had a vision for the mission field and felt that God had called him to serve in China, where he intended to go as soon as he graduated. He told me about a girl in the junior class—one of the most beautiful and dedicated Christian girls he had ever met. Sounded like my type. I paid attention.

One day we were hanging around in our sweaty work clothes in front of Williston Hall, the girls' dorm, getting ready to haul some furniture for a lady in Glen Ellyn, the next town over, when Johnny let out a whoop. "Billy, here's the girl I was telling you about," he said. "It's Ruth Bell."

I straightened up, and there she was. Standing there, looking right at me, was a slender, hazel-eyed movie starlet! I said something polite, but I was flustered and embarrassed. It took me a month to muster the courage to ask her out for a date.

The Christmas holidays were fast approaching, and the combined glee clubs were presenting Handel's *Messiah*. One day in the library in Blanchard Hall, I saw Ruth studying at one of the long tables. Johnny Streater and Howard Van Buren urged me to make my pitch to her right there. The expression of the librarian at the desk turned to a frown as we whispered among ourselves. Undaunted, I sauntered nonchalantly across to Ruth and scribbled my proposal for a date to the concert. To my surprise and delight, she agreed to go.

That Sunday afternoon was cold and snowy. With Ruth Bell sitting beside me in Pierce Chapel, I did not pay much attention to the music. Afterward we walked over to the Lane house for a cup of tea, and we had a chance to talk. I just could not believe that anyone could be so spiritual and so beautiful at one and the same time.

If I had not been smitten with love at the first sight of Ruth Bell, I would certainly have been the exception. Many of the men at Wheaton thought she was stunning. Petite, vivacious, smart, talented, witty, stylish, amiable, and unattached. What more could a fellow ask for?

I fell so head-over-heels in love with her that Johnny had to caution me. "You're going too fast."

And there was one minor problem that kept coming up. She wanted me to go with her as a missionary to Tibet! My mind was not closed to such a possibility. Not completely. After all, I had chosen to major in anthropology with just such a contingency in mind. But missionary work was a lot more comfortable to consider in the global abstract than in the Tibetan concrete.

In that list of good adjectives I just assigned to Ruth, I omitted one: determined.

She felt that God had called her to be a missionary to the remote borders of Tibet just as strongly as I felt that He had called me to preach the Gospel. In my case, though, there was not a geographical stipulation.

Ruth was deeply impressed by the life of Amy Carmichael, that single and indeed singular woman whom God had called to devote herself utterly to the children of Dohnavur, in southern India.

She reinforced her case by telling me about Mildred Cable, who had rejected the young man she loved because marriage to him would have cut across her call from God to do pioneer work in China.

Two things I felt sure of. First, that Ruth was bound to get married someday; and second, that I was the man she would marry. Beyond that, I did not try to pressure her or persuade her—that is to say, not overly much. I let God do my courting for me.

But as the months went by, I asked her to at least consider me. It would not have been right to let her assume that what seemed to be my heroic understanding of her concerns was a lack of interest or expectation on my part. We had lots of discussions about our relationship. I wouldn't call them arguments exactly, but we certainly did not see eye to eye.

In the meantime, Ruth enjoyed the social life at Wheaton, as I did, with many friends. One day she went canoeing on the Fox River in St. Charles, about ten miles west of Wheaton, with classmates Harold Lindsell, Carl Henry, and Carl's fiancée, Helga. Somehow the canoe capsized, and Ruth went under. Since both men were staunch Baptists, I suspected them of wanting to immerse the pretty Presbyterian missionary kid from China!

Because I was already an ordained Baptist minister, our divided denominational allegiance was another topic of conversation between us. Ruth stuck to her convictions.

"We've both got such strong wills or minds or something, I almost despaired of ever having things go peacefully between us," she wrote to her parents, "but I wouldn't want him any other way, and I can't be any other way. But you know, it's remarkable how two strong minds (or wills) like that can gradually begin to sort of fuse together. Or maybe we're learning to give in and don't realize it."

I was making some adjustments, certainly. At the Lane house one evening, I was so busy talking at the supper table that I ate three helpings of macaroni and cheese before I woke up to the fact that I had told Ruth I hated macaroni and cheese. That incident encouraged her to hope she could feed me anything and get away with it!

One Sunday evening after church, I walked into the parlor of the Gerstung home, where I was rooming, and collapsed into a chair. That dear professor of German and his wife, with three young boys of their own, were getting accustomed to my moods and always listened patiently. This time I bemoaned the fact that I did not stand a chance with Ruth. She was so superior to me in culture and poise.

By now I had directly proposed marriage to Ruth, and she was struggling with her decision. At the same time, she encouraged me to keep an open mind about the alternative of my going to the mission field. She was coming to realize, though, that the Lord was not calling me in that direction.

One day I posed a question to Ruth point-blank: "Do you believe that God brought us together?"

She thought so, without question.

"In that case," I said, "God will lead me, and you'll do the following."

She did not say yes to my proposal right then and there, but I
knew she was thinking it over.

A test of our bond came when
her sister Rosa was diagnosed as
having tuberculosis. Ruth dropped
out of school in the middle of my
second semester to care for her.

That summer I returned home
and preached in several churches
in the South. While I was in
Florida, preaching in Dr. Minder's
church, I got a thick letter from
Ruth postmarked July 6, 1941. One of the first sentences made me ecstatic, and I took off running. "I'll marry you," she wrote.

When I went back to my room, I read that letter over and over until church time. On page after page, Ruth explained how the Lord had worked in her heart and said she felt He wanted her to marry me. That night I got up to the pulpit and preached. When I finished and sat down, the pastor turned to me.

"Do you know what you just said?" he asked.

"No," I confessed.

"I'm not sure the people did either!"

After I went to bed, I switched my little lamp on and off all night, rereading that letter probably another dozen times.

(from Just As I Am)

GETTING TO KNOW EACH OTHER

Ruth and Billy Meet

Mother and Daddy were at Wheaton College when they met. Mother remembers seeing a tall young man on the stairs and said, "Well, there's a man in a hurry," and it's been that way ever since. She also remembers hearing him pray and thinking to herself, *That man knows to whom he is speaking.*

— GIGI GRAHAM TCHIVIDJIAN

Difficulties along the Way

I remember some of the difficulties Billy had in making progress with her. I remember she told me Billy had gotten very serious and wanted her to marry him and she wasn't sure. Finally, he said, "Ruth, I'm not going to date you for such and such a time. I'm just going to pray about it. I've asked you and I feel that's what the Lord wants and I'm just going to wait and see what He shows you." She told me that and asked me to pray with her about it.

I was standing in line for the dining hall one night and one of the young men said, "Hey, Rosa, I heard that your sister is going out with Billy Graham." I responded, "I guess so, once in a while." And he asked, "Well, what do you think of it?" I answered, "I don't know, I think we ought to pray about it." He said, "Nobody prayed for me when I dated her; I'm sure not going to be praying for Billy Graham." I thought that was hilarious and I just laughed and laughed and didn't say anything more.

— ROSA BELL MONTGOMERY

Ruth Meets the In-Laws

The first thing Billy told us about Ruth was how much she looked like our mother. Back then Ruth used to wear her hair in a bun and so did my mother. And when he brought Ruth down to Charlotte, she did remind all of us of Mother.

We all loved her and she is the best thing that ever happened to Billy. Absolutely the best thing.

—JEAN GRAHAM FORD

Learning When to Disagree

Before we were married, Bill was pastor of a little church in Wheaton, and they gave us a shower before we were married. The shower consisted of little sayings on pieces of paper. The best one, the one I've never forgotten, is that if two people agree on everything, one of them is unnecessary.

The important thing is to know when to disagree. You never disagree when tired or preoccupied or sleepy. That doesn't leave us much time. . . . [Laughs.] Never disagree with your hair up in rollers. Try to look as nice as you can. Tone of voice is very important. Rules of courtesy are very important.

See, I come from a long line of strong-minded, hardheaded individuals. Some people are much more flexible, milder, I would say, so there were times . . . but we celebrate our fiftieth [now almost sixty] this August.

—RUTH BELL GRAHAM, IN AN INTERVIEW WITH WESLEY PIPPERT

Adjustments

In addition to Ruth's [preparing for the wedding, she was] finishing up her senior year at college. But I too had schoolwork to finish, and I think she was exasperated by the fact that I was on the road so often. After telling her folks about my coming itinerary in Flint, Michigan; Rockford, Illinois; and then "Wisconsin or Pennsylvania or somewhere," she wrote, "I can't keep control of him much less keep track of him."

Already she sensed the kind of future we faced together. "I'm a rotten sport when it comes to his leaving. It's no fun. I never thought about this side of it. What's it going to be like after we're married? I probably won't see as much of him as I do now."

Something loomed immediately ahead, though, that made Ruth and me both expect me to stay put a little more.

One day a big Lincoln Continental pulled up in front of the house where I was rooming. Out of it popped a young man who bounded up the steps and asked to see me. . . . His name was Bob Van Kampen, and he wanted to sound me out about becoming pastor of the church where he was a deacon, Western Springs Baptist Church, about twenty miles southeast of Wheaton.

In January 1943, midway through my senior year, I began to feel the responsibility of supporting a wife. . . . Hence, I accepted the call to Western Springs; I had already preached there as a student, and I could begin work there after college commencement. In my enthusiasm, however, I forgot to consult my bride-to-be! She let me know in no uncertain terms that she did not appreciate such insensitivity. And I could not blame her.

—BILLY GRAHAM, *Just As I Am*

Chapter Five

BILLY, PART TWO (MARRIED LIFE)

When two people agree about everything, one of them is unnecessary.
—ONE OF RUTH BELL GRAHAM'S FAVORITE QUOTES

THE WEDDING
BILLY GRAHAM

*R*uth's parents had moved from Virginia to a house on the Presbyterian conference grounds at Montreat, North Carolina, just east of Asheville. We were married there in August, on the night of Friday the thirteenth, with a full moon in the sky. In Gaither Chapel at eight-thirty in the evening. It was the most memorable day of my life.

For a wedding present, my father had already given me fifty dollars. I had twenty-five dollars of my own saved up. That meant I had seventy-five dollars to pay for a honeymoon and get us back to Chicago.

The first night we went to the Battery Park Hotel in Asheville; that cost us five dollars for the night. I had wanted Ruth to have the best, but the Grove Park Inn would have cost twenty dollars. I couldn't sleep in the bed, so after Ruth fell asleep, I got up quietly, lay down on the floor, and dropped right off. (I had suffered from insomnia all through school, and Chief Whitefeather, who had come through town once and given his Christian testimony, had suggested that I sleep on the floor. He promised that though it would take a couple of weeks to get used to, it would help my problem, and he was right.) The next morning, when Ruth woke up, I was gone . . . or at least appeared to be gone. It took a few minutes for her to find me on the floor, sleeping like a baby.

We then drove to Boone, where we went to a private home that let out rooms; ours cost one dollar. To get to the bathroom at night, we had to go through two other rooms where people were sleeping. At the end of our stay, Ruth confided in the lady of the house that we were on our honeymoon.

"Yes, I know," she said. "I've been sweeping up the rice every day."

We ate out at little sandwich places and played golf: Ruth knew nothing about the game, and I knew little more, in spite of the cad-dying I had done in Florida. There were many people behind us on the course each time, and we did not know we were supposed to let them play through.

One time we decided to splurge. We ate a meal at Mayview Manor, the place to eat in town. Lunch was three dollars. My money was going fast. But we decided, just for one night, to spend two dollars at the Boone Hotel.

Then we went back to my family's home in Charlotte, but there was no room for us. My sister Catherine was getting married; Jean had a room, and so did Melvin. So we slept on the floor in what my mother called her sunroom.

Our trip back to Chicago, after our brief honeymoon in the Blue Ridge Mountains near home, was uneventful.

(from *Just As I Am*)

Ruth and Billy's Wedding

At the wedding she was beautiful, absolutely beautiful. She made her own dress and most of her trousseau, and everything was just lovely. She had the dearest friends she could ever expect to have as part of the wedding. It was a really happy occasion.

—ROSA BELL MONTGOMERY

Ruth has been my sister-in-law almost sixty years. I can't think of anything that I would want in a sister-in-law that I don't have in her.

I remember the day they got married very well. I was eleven years old. They got married in Montreat, which is a Presbyterian confer-ence center. I wanted to spend all day long with Ruth—and I did. They made all their own flower arrangements out of wildflowers and I helped do that. I'm sure I was in the way, but she was so gracious.

—JEAN GRAHAM FORD

Being Married to Bill

Ruth Bell Graham

*R*uth's explanation to those who asked how she coped with his travel was, "I'd rather have Bill part-time than anybody else full-time."

⁓

Looking back, being married to anybody but Bill might be boring. There were times when I envied—not really envied, because I think that is the wrong word—wives who have their husbands at home more, and a more normal, more usual sort of life.

I just thank God for the privilege that He has allowed me to be married to the man that I think is the finest man I know. So it has been a privilege to share him with the rest of the world. It's not always easy, but God never promised easy.

There have been times when I wished we could have him at home more. Especially, this has been hard on the children and it has been hard on him, although I don't think he realizes how much he missed seeing them as they were growing up.

I remember Anne, when she was little, sitting out in the yard and a plane went overhead. I saw her look up and wave her little hands and say, "Bye, Daddy! Bye, Daddy!" I guess she just associated planes with her daddy.

I don't think the children remember the absences as much as they remember the times when he was home, and each one has happy memories of their father. He is a very caring person, and I think when they were little they thought that everybody's father traveled.

I tell you, if I didn't have God and know He was there with me,

I couldn't have managed. And also, our wonderful friends. We live in a unique community. It used to be mainly for retired ministers and retired missionaries. We had the kindest neighbors.

The important thing, if a man feels like God has called him on the road, is to settle his wife where she would be the happiest. In some places I don't think I could have made it, but at the time Mother and Daddy lived across the road, and we lived right next door.

Billy Graham's longtime right-hand man, T. W. Wilson, describes Ruth's influence on Billy in this way: "There would have been no Billy Graham as we know him today had it not been for Ruth."

(from *Hindsights*)

SEEKING MOTHER'S ADVICE

ANNE GRAHAM LOTZ

*M*y daddy didn't have to seek my mother's advice to get it.

I remember a time she tells about him just fussing at her because he just didn't want her opinion. He does not like opinionated women and he has a house full of them. He didn't want her opinion and she said she would be ashamed to admit that she married someone whose opinion he couldn't take. My mother is very feisty and whether he asked for her opinion or not, believe you me, she gave it.

I have three children and each of them has been married a few years. I've watched as the girls learned to become wives and the guys learned to become husbands. It takes awhile for a man who's been living independently to take on this partner and consult her. He's not used to doing that. I think in some of those stories, Daddy was just learning to be a husband. I don't think he meant to do it in a rude way or he didn't want her opinion, but he wasn't used to doing that. That's not what he'd seen. But my mother set him straight on that. Today he would not only consult her opinion, he would respect it and honor it and listen to her. She has enormous wisdom.

I remember being in Switzerland one year and overhearing that a group had put pressure on Daddy to put his name in nomination for the presidency of the United States. It was a group of people who were willing to fund his candidacy. My mother was so clear. She said, "When God calls you to be an evangelist, you don't stoop to be president."

She didn't let him get sidetracked for a moment, and she has kept him focused. When other people might have put pressure on this or that, she was right there as rock-solid in confirming his call as anybody.

I don't believe the world would have a Billy Graham if it weren't for a Ruth Bell Graham. I think it has taken the two of them to do what's been done. And I'm very grateful to see them up close and personal and see the consistency in their lives.

Someone asked John Wayne's son, "What's the real John Wayne like?" He answered, "There's not two John Waynes." I'd say the same of Daddy. What's the real Billy Graham like? The real Billy Graham is the one you see. There aren't two of them. That's been a blessing to watch—the reality of their faith lived out on the anvil of those day-to-day experiences of the things that go wrong. To have done it so well and to maintain the consistency of their faith and their joy in the Lord and their love for other people—it's amazing. That's God's grace.

My mother will tell you she was never lonely when Daddy was gone, sometimes as much as nine out of twelve months. She will tell you looking back she doesn't remember loneliness in that way. She will tell you that she missed him and I know she would sometimes go to sleep with his jacket.

I know my mother and daddy—one of the blessings is that they've been so in love. We all knew that, but her life was so full with raising five kids and all those responsibilities. I know there is a loneliness that comes out in her poetry, but it's a loneliness that turned her to God. What my mother passed on to me, more than anything else, was that her relationship with God was personal and fresh. And she spent time in God's Word. That's where she would know Jesus. And Jesus met that loneliness and that need for companionship in her life. I never, ever heard my mother complain.

I never heard her say, "Billy, why are you going off again? You just came back! You mean you're leaving me again with all these kids?" Never did I ever hear her fuss or complain or express resentment, never. Mother was always totally supportive and I don't think she put it on for us. That was in her heart. And I believe God called my mother just as clearly as he called my daddy—called her to world evangelism but she expressed the call by staying home, taking care of us, freeing my daddy up to answer that same call but by leaving home being the evangelist that the world's known. I believe God called them together, the both of them.

They expressed their obedience to that call in two different ways and made a complete package. So my mother really freed my daddy to live and serve almost as a single person. He had a wife and children but she freed him up from the responsibility and entanglements that a family sometimes brings and the limits it puts on what someone can do, just because of their family responsibility. And she freed him from all that so he could give himself totally to what God had him to do and yet also have the blessing of a family.

MARRIAGE ADJUSTMENTS

Ruth and Billy Graham have not found marriage to be an easy merger. A different culture, a different outlook on the world, and different challenges separated Ruth Bell from Billy Graham. She grew up as a missionary's child in China, he on a dairy farm in North Carolina. Only one thing brought them together—their faith in God.

The most difficult adjustment for Ruth in the early years of their marriage was learning to live with a man who had grown up in a family where the women did not take much part in the conversation. "In my family, women were very outspoken," Ruth said. "I had to learn with Bill that when I spoke, I should speak with more wisdom."

"My home life was so different," she added. "We were missionaries so we had to depend upon each other for company. In the evenings we took turns reading through the classics. Bill was more of a country boy."

—JULIE NIXON EISENHOWER, *Special People*

A Steely Will

She not only was used to speaking up and joining in the conversation, but also she had the kind of steely will that enabled her to resist the pressure from his family and friends who insisted that the Graham children be raised as Baptists. "They were not raised as Baptists. Or Presbyterians," Ruth told me. "They were raised as Christians."

—JULIE NIXON EISENHOWER

Leaving

There were a lot of times I went down the driveway at home with tears in my eyes because I didn't want to go. I knew it would be days or weeks before I would see her again.

—BILLY GRAHAM

Adoration and Respect

Ruth is a powerful, strong, intelligent, interesting woman, and you cannot miss that when you are around her. But when Billy walks into the room, something happens. The dynamic between them was very interesting to watch. They both love, adore, and respect each other.

—ANDIE MacDOWELL

Both of Us Married Very Strong Men

Both of us married very strong men and grew into the wife of someone who belongs to the world. And I just think it is startlingly happy that Ruth and Billy found each other and wound up together.

But the people who found each other at a young age were not the same people as twenty or thirty years later because they had each had an effect on the other. They have sort of grown together. And it's a good thing for the country and the world that they were willing to let life work on them.

The life Billy has lived must have been filled with needful people, and he must have needed to put his head on the pillow and relax. Ruth provided him with peace and was a true person to spend the hours with.

—CLAUDIA (LADY BIRD) JOHNSON

Home Can Be a Place to Recharge the Battery

I try to arrange things so that, when he's home, there's no particular crises. I think it's very important when a busy, tired man comes home that his needs be catered to. In other words, home can be a place where he recharges his battery. How you handle this depends entirely on the temperament of the man. Some husbands relax better with company and people to talk to; others relax better working out in the yard; others relax better with television. So when Bill comes home, he calls the shots. We only have company when he wants to have company, unless it is really an exceptional case. He does what he feels he needs to do. He has an awful lot of work piled up when he comes home—correspondence and so forth.

—RUTH BELL GRAHAM, IN AN INTERVIEW WITH WESLEY PIPPERT

Fighting and Arguing

I never heard them fight or disagree. And in some ways that was a negative thing. I know one of my sisters had an argument soon after she was married and thought the marriage was over because she had not seen Mother and Daddy really argue. I know they disagreed, and being their daughter I could tell when certain looks or certain facial expressions were made. She did that recently with her walker, and I thought, *Oh no, we're in trouble now.*

—GIGI GRAHAM TCHIVIDJIAN

If they have fought, I don't know about it. I can't imagine that there hasn't been, but I just don't know about it.

—JEAN GRAHAM FORD

I think of Ruth Bell Graham as almost the perfect woman. Perfect because she's got a sense of humor and such family loyalty. And I love her because she says what she thinks. I've enjoyed our friendship.

I love her support of Billy. To me it is so important to support your husband, your children, and your friends. And Ruth has been very supportive to us.

—BARBARA BUSH

Chapter Six

FAMILY

Bringing up a family should be an adventure, not anxious discipline in which everybody is constantly graded for performance.
— MILTON R. SAPIRSTEIN, *Paradoxes of Everyday Life*

I'VE BEEN TOLD I WAS "QUITE A HANDFUL"
FRANKLIN GRAHAM

*M*y daddy's father was named William Franklin Graham. He was called Frank. My father was born on November 7, 1918, and named William Franklin Graham II. He was called Billy Frank by his family and close friends in his hometown of Charlotte, North Carolina.

When I arrived on the scene July 14, 1952, my parents appropriately named me William Franklin Graham III. To cut down on further confusion, Mama and Daddy decided to call me Franklin.

My parents lived in Montreat, North Carolina, a small community about fifteen miles east of Asheville. In my opinion, it's one of the most beautiful spots on earth—in the heart of the Blue Ridge Mountains. For as long as I can remember, these mountains and wooded hills of western Carolina have been the only place I ever wanted to call home.

As a young boy, I had no idea that my father was well-known. As with any kid, he was just "Daddy" to me. I'm told that by the time I was three, tourists were finding their way to Montreat and beginning to poke around our house, which sat on the main road. Every now and then, caravans of cars would pull up and stop in front of our house. People would climb out to gawk and snap pictures. Those who were brave would walk to the front door and try to peek in through the windows.

My older sisters, who apparently were quite the entrepreneurs, saw a business opportunity. They set up a lemonade stand and sold "Billy Graham's favorite lemonade" to the tourists for five cents a glass.

It wasn't too long before my folks bought 150 acres of heavily wooded mountain land outside of Montreat. The rear of the property bordered thousands of acres that were part of the Asheville reservoir's watershed, known as the North Fork, so it was an ideal location for a family needing some seclusion and space. Mama named it "Little Piney Cove." I call it "home."

I don't think she ever talked about him leaving. We knew he was preaching, but we thought everyone's father was away a lot. It's just something we grew up with. She was always positive and would quote the old mountain man: "Make least of all that goes, most of all that comes."

I've been told that I was "quite a handful" when I was a kid.

Most boys love to explore, learn how things work, and experiment—I certainly was no different. I was just being me.

While Mama talked to the foreman and workers, I found creative ways to entertain myself. I stayed right on the heels of the carpenters, watching their every move. The thing they did that intrigued me most was smoking. I was fascinated by it. I caught on that if I ran quick enough when they pitched a cigarette, the butt would still be lit. I would grab one and puff away, thinking no one would notice.

Out of nowhere, of course, would come Mama. She'd grab the cigarette out of my mouth and fling it away. "No, Franklin!" She would lecture me on all the evils of smoking, but that didn't stop me. I just got more clever at not getting caught. The workmen thought it was funny and would purposely throw a half-smoked cigarette in my direction, hoping I would pick it up. Then they would watch to see if Mama would catch me.

I remember one day after lunch a carpenter lit up, took a big drag, and blew the smoke down a piece of pipe. I was on the other end and sucked it all in. About that time Mama came into the room. When she saw what was going on, she was madder than a hornet. She jerked that pipe out of his hand—I thought she was going to whip him with it. Needless to say, he never did that again.

This was the beginning of what later became a bad habit for me.

The entire family was relieved when we finally moved into our new yet old-looking log home. Although it was very comfortable and modern, because of the old logs and the antique furniture Mama had found, the home looked like it might have been built a hundred years earlier.

I especially loved playing outside in all the open space at Little Piney Cove, often pretending I was Matt Dillon from *Gunsmoke* or one of the Cartwright brothers from *Bonanza*. I had a complete set of cowboy gear—boots, jeans, shirt, hat, and most importantly, a holster and pistol. I would dress up in my cowboy duds and play in the woods for hours.

I was fascinated with toy guns—I guess because in my mind it was the closest I had to the real thing at age four. Mama recalls that shortly after we moved up to the log house, I persuaded her to let me camp out on the front porch. When she checked up on me the next morning, there I was on a camp cot, fully dressed in my jeans, denim jacket, and boots—with my toy gun propped against the side of the cot. As Mama tells the story:

"How did you sleep last night?" I asked him.

"Fine," Franklin said.

"And you weren't afraid of the skunk?" (One had visited us the night before.)

"No, ma'am," he replied, "I had my gun with me."

"But Franklin, it's just a toy gun."

He looked at me with a twinkle in his eye and said, "Polecat didn't know it!"

Of course Mama and Daddy insisted that I behave, but I had a very strong will. I suppose I wasn't a horrible child, but I definitely had a rebellious streak. When I wanted to do something, I did it—

even if I knew I would be disobeying my parents and risking punishment. And I found real delight in avoiding getting caught or flaunting my rebellious ways. This would all catch up with me later.

My habit of finding cigarette butts and smoking them got so bad that when Floyd Roberts, our caretaker, came up to the house one evening to see how everything was, Mama asked to borrow the pack of cigarettes he was carrying in his pocket.

"I'm going to teach Franklin a lesson," she told Floyd.

She brought me into the kitchen and sat me down in front of the fireplace. *What is she up to?* I wondered.

She opened the pack, pulled out a cigarette, and handed it to me. "Now light it and smoke it—and be sure to inhale!" Mama wanted me to get sick, thinking that if I threw up I would never want to touch a cigarette again.

I couldn't believe Mama was actually giving me permission to smoke! I remembered Daddy telling me how his daddy whipped the taste right out of his mouth when he was a boy after Granddaddy caught him smoking—and it had worked! So I was surprised that Mama was actually letting me smoke with her blessing. This was great.

"Sure," I said, and lit the first cigarette and inhaled deeply.

Mama watched as I puffed, her face expressionless. "Keep smoking," she said.

I did. When I finished the second one, my face turned as green as a cow's cud. I ran into the bathroom and threw up. I washed my face and headed back to the kitchen for more. I picked up the third cigarette, and with a cocky grin, struck the match and went at it again. Within minutes, I raced back to the bathroom to puke again. I wasn't easily deterred.

By the time I had finished all twenty, I must have vomited five or six times. I felt horrible. Every time I got sick, I'm sure Mama thought her approach was working, but it gave me great satisfaction not to give in. That wasn't the result Mama wanted.

I wasn't sure my stomach would ever stop churning. But if there had been another pack of cigarettes, I probably would have smoked them too!

Mama didn't give up trying to make me quit smoking, but she never used that tactic again.

In those days, we didn't know the health dangers involved with smoking. As a kid, I probably wouldn't have cared anyway. I can still see those carpenters with cigarettes dangling from their lips, the smoke rising in tiny clouds above them. To me it was cool. Most of these guys were World War II veterans; they were my heroes. You couldn't help but look up to and admire them.

(from *Rebel with a Cause*)

KID STORIES

BETTY FRIST

A former secretary of Ruth's who, at the time, lived in the Graham home, kept notes as to what went on among the little Grahams and shared some of the stories with me as well as with Ruth and Billy.

Little Anne said, "I know there is a Santa Claus 'cause I got a bracelet for Christmas that must have cost at least two dollars. And I know Mommie and Daddy couldn't afford that!"

Franklin spoke of "Menace the Dentist."

When Gigi went to Hampton DuBose School the first time, she carried in her suitcase an ample supply of socks. A few days later, she telephoned to ask her mother if she would send more socks. "What happened to all the socks you took with you?" inquired Ruth. "They're dirty," came the reply.

Once, when Ruth was out of town, Bunny told her grandmother on the phone that she wanted to come down to the valley for the night. "I know about everything on this mountain, and I'm looking for new places to sleep."

One day I walked into the kitchen and found Franklin playing with matches. "Franklin, you know your daddy told you not to play with matches," I scolded. "No, he didn't," insisted Franklin. "He told me not to let him catch me playing with matches." Then he said with a grin, "And I'm not going to let him catch me." After delivering a little sermon, I asked, "Don't you think you should confess this to him?" "Heck, no!" replied Franklin. "He'd beat the dickens out of me."

Anne and her friend had seen the film *Tonka*. On the way home, I heard the most delightful conversation that went something like this:

Anne: "Did you see those muscles?"
Friend: "Whose? Sal Mineo's?"
Anne: "Oh, no! I meant the horse's."

When Ruth (Bunny) heard someone talking about Miss America, she asked, "Who is Miss America? Is she Uncle Sam's wife?"

(from *My Neighbors, the Billy Grahams*)

On Raising Children
Ruth Bell Graham

I never came up to the pattern Mother and Daddy set for me, due partly to the kind of life we've had to lead. We've had more distractions. And television, although I think it's a tremendous boon in many ways, is a great handicap in others. We haven't played as many games together in the evening, for example. My family was a great one for games.

The very first thing in raising children is to be the woman that God wants me to be, and this is where I have fallen so far short. Now, this verse came to me this summer after Franklin had taken off for London. When you send a nineteen-year-old boy to pick up a Land Rover in London and drive it to Jordan, well, I was praying! And I was reading John 17, which I had read on other occasions, as my prayer for the children. This was our Lord's prayer before He died, as He was leaving His disciples behind. Only in this case, the child was leaving me, not the other way around. Still, the prayer was very appropriate. Any mother could read it for her children. The verse that really hit me between the eyes was the nineteenth, where Jesus says, "For their sake I consecrate myself that they also may be truly consecrated."

If our Lord needed to pray that prayer, how much more do we parents for our children's sake? We can't expect them to be truly committed if we aren't. This is where so many of us fall flat on our faces. We're great at preaching, but we're terribly weak on the practicing part. I think how often I have failed my kids on this. I expected more of them spiritually than I was willing to give myself. The important thing is to be what God wants us to be. If I were the type of person God wanted me to be, 90 percent of the problems in the family would be solved.

I'm afraid—and this is a confession—I'm not a good disciplinarian, to the children's detriment. A good disciplinarian is someone who disciplines consistently, no matter how he or she feels. If I'm really tired, I usually just give in on a point if the children press it. Or, if I get really upset, I'm likely to be too strict with them when I shouldn't have been. I think a good disciplinarian is much more objective and consistent than that. Because Bill has been gone much of the time, I have loved the children not wisely but too well. I get emotionally involved, and sometimes I'm inclined to be more lenient with them, thinking I have to make up for the fact their father is not here, when really they would like me to be a little tougher with them.

One day when we were out in California, our thirteen-year-old was getting out of hand, and I was chewing him out.

"Now listen," I said, "you've got to realize that I've been pretty lenient with you on this trip."

"That's the trouble, Mom," he said. "You should have been more strict."

I don't think this is unusual. Kids appreciate discipline. So when I say that I have been too lenient, I wish I hadn't been. I wish I had been stricter.

If Billy had been home consistently he would have been a tremendous disciplinarian. This is the ideal in a family, I think, when the father can be the disciplinarian, and the mother can relax and just be sweet and loving. But when the father is gone most of the time, the mother has to be disciplinarian as well.

(from an interview with Wesley Pippert)

THE HARDEST AND MOST IMPORTANT JOB IN THE WORLD

JULIE NIXON EISENHOWER

*R*uth Graham chose to have five children. Both the Grahams are convinced that a mother's job is the "hardest and most important job in the world." Ruth believes that the real liberation mothers need is to be freed from the burden of working outside the home. She does not believe motherhood can be a part-time job. "A mother, like God, must be a very present help in time of trouble," she told me. "Children do not wait until five-thirty in the afternoon to encounter a problem."

"But what about women who have to work?" I asked.

She had a ready answer. "Children are perceptive," she said. "They know if their mother is working for an extra color television or because the family cannot do without the money she earns."

"What about those women who feel they do not have the patience to stay home all day long with small children?"

Ruth unblinkingly said, "I believe one can learn to be patient."

One almost has to be sitting next to Ruth as I was when she expresses these opinions. Otherwise she sounds rigid and, given the aspirations of women today, unrealistic. But when she describes being a mother, she is so earnest. She does not feel she denied herself during the years she spent with her children. She looks at a woman's life as a matter of timing—with different roles at different stages. Today, now that her children are grown, she has time for the poetry, painting, and sewing she enjoys. She has the freedom to travel with her husband. As she talked, I was more aware than I had been before that her tanned face, although still youthful, is deeply lined. The lines seemed evidence of the struggle of bearing and almost single-handedly raising five children. But it was a struggle that Ruth clearly gloried in. I sensed no hint of regret.

Ruth feels there is no institution more worth fighting for than the family. The fight is difficult because the parents, two completely different people, must try to function as a single unit. In the words of the Bible, man and wife become "one flesh." Ruth describes marriage as a triangle: God at the top, with husband and wife on the same plane on the bottom. While the husband has certain responsibilities in the home and, in Ruth's view, final authority, and the wife other responsibilities, marriage is not a question of lording it over each other; it is a question of giving in to each other.

(from *Special People*)

FAMILY LIFE

We Grew Up with Daddy Being Gone

We grew up with Daddy being gone. I really don't have memories of my mother trying to compensate for my dad's not being there. Mother just didn't make a big deal of it. He's been at all the high school graduations and weddings and grandchildren's weddings. So that's been special.

—GIGI GRAHAM TCHIVIDJIAN

Coming Home

I remember coming home one time and we went to bed. At this time there was a small trundle bed under the bed and occasionally one of the children would sleep there. On this particular night, when Franklin was a little boy, he came out of the trundle bed, saw me in bed, and asked his mother, "Mama, who is that in bed with you?"

Then I began to wonder if she had others in here. I didn't really wonder; I just made a joke of it.

—BILLY GRAHAM

When Daddy Left

My mother once again was very wise. And when Daddy left, she sort of ignored the leaving. We didn't make a big deal of it. I would go to school and when I came home he was gone. It was a casual, ho-hum, so he's gone again. When he came home it was a big deal. And we all went to the railroad station. There was a big celebration when he came home. He always had gifts for us. Looking back, I know they were just things he picked up at the airport or train station, nothing wonderful, but we always knew Daddy would have a prize for us. We would dive through the suitcase to look for the prize, and he did that probably until I went off and got married. He always brought me a prize or something from his trips. Now I do the same thing for my children even though they're married and out of the house.

Also, when he stepped in the door, there was no question who was in authority. I don't know how my mother did that. She was definitely the boss when he wasn't there, and she was the one who disciplined us and all that, but when he walked in the door that adjusted and he was in control. He was in charge and when he said jump, we just asked how high. I never ever in my life thought of contradicting my daddy or talking back to him or saying no if he asked me to do something. And yet he was very gentle, very affectionate, very loving, fun with us as children, but very much the one that had the respect and authority within the home.

—ANNE GRAHAM LOTZ

Mother and Daddy Were Protective about Publicity

Mother and Daddy were very protective about publicity. I would never have been able to give an interview like this growing up. Never allowed to be interviewed by the print press and TV. They shielded us from all of that.

I can read things about Daddy now, but I wouldn't have known that was going on in his life. He was just our daddy who was gone a lot. But we lived a very normal life. On one hand, I missed a lot of what he was experiencing. On the other hand, I believe my parents made the right choices because it meant that I grew up normally, with a good perspective, and I wouldn't take anything for that.

—ANNE GRAHAM LOTZ

Chapter Seven

North Carolina

Give me a cove
—a little cove—
when Fall comes
amblin' round.
—Ruth Bell Graham

THE LONG AND WINDING ROAD
BETTY FRIST

*I*f you're planning to look for the Billy Graham property, you may end up wishing you'd stayed home because it's at the end of a scalloped, tortuous mountain road, sometimes called "Coronary Hill." Your car will strain up and up and around like a broken arrow. Chipmunks scurry across the road in front of the car. It's no place for nervous people. A nearby resident says, "I've personally seen two cars with their front ends hanging off into space."

But if you're still determined to find it, keep going until "the air gets thin, your nose begins to bleed, and you see buzzards circling," and you'll eventually come on a gate with a sign politely suggesting, "Please turn around here." Of course, the Grahams must maintain their family privacy, of which they have little as a rule.

In 1950 the Grahams bought their approximately two hundred acres on top of the mountain for $4,500. That was in the days before land sold by the square inch and a person owning a grave plot was considered a land baron.

Beyond the gate a visitor will pass two little cabins that were on the place when it was bought. One has stodgy, whimsical little fantasy figures on faded blue shutters painted by Ruth. This cabin has an L-shaped room, a fireplace, a loft, and a path leading outside. The cabin is completely dehydrated—there was never any running water unless a child ran with a bucket of water from the spring. The other cabin is a little larger, but is fed with water from one of the eighteen springs on the mountain.

One summer Ruth offered one of the cabins to a friend to vacation in, writing in her inimitable way, "Now what's wrong with the little old cabin? Provided the water's turned on, the dead mice fished out of the tub (two in there now), the septic tank doesn't leak all over the place, and no more than six people are squashed in at one time?"

The next description sounded more captivating. "Spring in all its glory is here. Everywhere you look is shimmering chartreuse, bowers of white dogwood, apple blossoms, and violets underfoot. The mountains are brilliant now. This cove is a dream."

About this time, a friend received a letter from Ruth informing her, "We're seriously considering moving up the mountain in another year. For good. Most of the leaves are gone now and you can see— and it's wonderful. Forty bushels of apples are stored in the apple cellar and ten times that many are tempting the bears and yellow jackets as they rot. The spring is just as strong and the little cabin cuter 'n ever—bushels of black walnuts this year and everything tinder dry. The men say there have been bear tracks around the spring." (Ruth goes hunting for a three-hundred-pound bear armed with a camera loaded with film, and Ruth herself is loaded with raw courage.)

Ruth is hooked on log cabins. She wrote, "All I want for my old age is a log cabin with a loft." She doesn't mean the round logs so often seen today but the ancient square-cut logs that were laboriously hewn out by hand with a tool called the broad axe and another one called an adz, which Ruth used to display on the mantel of the fireplace in their guest room.

The house is a layer and a half type and is constructed of this type of log cabin transplants. The cabins had long been on the critical list and were dismantled and brought to the building site.

To Ruth, there's something very special about these old logs which seem to almost pulsate with life. For over a century, they've absorbed and stored the pungent aroma of frying country ham and red eye gravy, freshly baked bread, and bracing hot coffee brewed from newly ground coffee beans. They've plucked from the air the sigh of the old hound dog snoozing by the fire, the low murmurings of lovers, the groans and piercing cries at childbirth, the sounds of muffled sobbing at death, the hoedown beat of the mountain music erupting from the cherished old handmade violins and guitars, and twanging of the musical saws as they formed the backdrop for the wildly gyrating feet of the square dancers. Laughter and prayer also penetrated these walls—all of which adds up to a host of memory flashbacks. The ancient logs and a sense of peace envelops you as you erase from your thoughts the seething chaos of today's living and replace it with the tranquil whisperings of days long gone and the simple joys that were part of those days. At times you feel a deep ache and an intense longing for the return of that shrouded distant past which you well know can live again only in memory.

Since Ruth had studied any cabins she could find still standing and pored over any books she could lay her hands on about log cabins, she wanted the chimney rocks in the old authentic dry rock fashion. She was willing to have cement used between the rocks for safety and stability, but she didn't want it to show. This was anathema to the twentieth-century rock mason who wanted the cement to upstage the rocks. Finally, in disgust, and with a look of loathing at his work done under Ruth's tutelage, he threw down his tools and walked off the job, saying, "A man can't take no pride in his work up here."

In another letter, Ruth expressed concern that she might have to lock horns with the architect. Ruth knew what she wanted, and when the architect was hesitant about incorporating one of her ideas into his plan, she stuck a pacifier into his mouth by saying, "I'll tell you what, Joe! So you won't get credit for my ideas, when the house is finished, I'll put up a sign in the yard saying, 'Joe Ware, Architect' and under it, 'Ruth Bell Graham, Counter-Architect!'"

(from *My Neighbors, the Billy Grahams*)

A Visit with the Grahams

Julie Nixon Eisenhower

*W*hen I visited the Grahams at their mountaintop home in Montreat in North Carolina, Ruth picked me up at the airport in Asheville after my "puddle-jump" flight from New York, which had made two stops before touching down in Asheville. Montreat is tucked away in the Black Mountains, not an easily accessible crossroads, despite the fact that it is the home of one of the most sought-after men in the world.

As we approached the house, Ruth used the radio intercom to let her husband know we were almost there. As soon as she had finished transmitting, Billy came on. "I know," he said. "We've been hearing a very interesting conversation for the last five minutes." The microphone had rolled into a crack between the car seats in such a way that the intercom button was depressed. The result was that no one could reach us and inform us that our chatter was being overheard. It must have been an amusing five minutes. Ruth and I had talked about the weather, the merits of several crusade staff members, and the arthritic problems of a mutual friend, which somehow had led to a discussion of hot flashes. When we learned that we had had an audience (the radio is also hooked up to aide T. W. Wilson's house) we laughed so hard that tears rolled out of the corners of my eyes. Ruth was doubled over the wheel and for a few seconds, despite the dizzying curves of the mountain road, she pumped the accelerator wildly because she could not stop laughing. We were still laughing when Ruth drove through the electronically controlled gate for the final climb up the steep, winding road to the house.

The Grahams' house is made of hand-hewn logs from old abandoned cabins. The world of commercialism and cynicism seemed remote in this corner of the Black Mountains. The kitchen is the heart of the house, a large room, its walls and ceilings, like those of all the other rooms, of exposed timber. A fire blazed on the open hearth. A colorful rag rug covered the brick floor and pewter jugs dented with years of use were hung on wooden pegs. It would be hard not to feel at home in the Grahams' kitchen. But the whole house was equally simple and welcoming. A hail window was filled with glass bottles. When I admired an especially pretty dark blue bottle, Ruth told me it was a Milk of Magnesia bottle minus its label.

The room I liked almost as much as the kitchen was my own, the spare bedroom. It invited a guest to relax, to sleep late—to be at peace. Everything was simple but designed for a guest's comfort. Ruth kept a coffeemaker on the closet shelf so that guests could have that first cup of coffee in the morning without having to dress and go to the kitchen. There was another braided rag rug on the wide-plank floor, and another fireplace with the logs laid ready for a match. On the chest of drawers beside the bed was a row of books including a history of China, several works by C. S. Lewis, and a *Daily Light,* which contains Scripture verses for each day of the year. Surprisingly there was no Bible.

My bed was huge—and high. I had to use a two-step wooden stair to climb in. I hoped that I would not be restless during the night. It would be a hard landing if I were to roll out of bed. Underneath was a trundle bed for the grandchildren. A koala bear and a green stuffed walrus were tucked away in the closet for their visits.

Ruth Graham's parents had settled in Montreat when they returned from China at the beginning of World War II. And because Billy traveled so much, Ruth chose to raise her children in this beautiful and peaceful community. It is the place, Billy says, where he most often finds renewal because he has more time when he is home to study the Bible and to think.

Everything is geared to Billy when he is in Montreat. Ruth

refuses to have a firm schedule when Billy is there. "Being married to Bill, I have to hang loose and play it by ear," she told me. And then she laughed, "I tell my friends I have become a very loose woman indeed!" The daily routine was carefully designed around her husband during my visit. On Saturday, we ate our large meal of the day at noon. Ruth and the caretaker's wife, who helps with the housework, did the cooking. But the rest of Saturday and all day Sunday we were completely alone enjoying the peace and privacy that Billy looks forward to so much on the weekends when he is home.

Their house in Montreat offers more than privacy to the Grahams. It offers physical security. They had to move out of the little town up to their mountaintop twenty years ago when it became impossible to cope with the tourists who would walk into the yard, take photographs of the children, even look in the windows. People often arrived at the front door demanding to see Billy and then were extremely unhappy, sometimes quite unpleasant, if, as was often the case, he was not at home. Their present property, which they bought for five dollars an acre, is surrounded by an eleven-foot-high fence, erected at the suggestion of the FBI after the assassination of Martin Luther King Jr., a time when there was an alarming increase in the number of threats on Billy Graham's life.

The fence, the dog, and the radio communications setup between car and home are all security precautions urged on the Grahams by concerned friends and staff. The Grahams themselves have a casual attitude toward it all. Ruth, in fact, jokes that her guardian angel is "highly insulted," especially by the fence. She and Billy tend to turn the security measures into toys, just as [their guard dogs] become rather lazy, sleep-by-the-fire pets.

The morning after I arrived, Ruth and I went for a hike before the onslaught of a threatening rain. With the dog and a marshmallow fork to protect us against copperheads and rattlesnakes, we climbed up the mountain behind their house. I had to concentrate so hard on the thorny blackberry bushes and the thick "touch-me-not" vines that became entangled around my feet and legs that I did not worry much about snakes. And anyway, Ruth had assured me that we would get a little warning—according to her mountain neighbor, Dad Roberts, snakes smell like cucumbers.

Ruth set a fast pace up an incline that seemed almost perpendicular to me. "Let me know when you want to stop to rest," she said. I was sure she would call a halt before I did, but finally, rather sheepishly, I suggested we sit for a while on a log in an opening that was just "too picturesque" to pass by. The aspens and maples still had their leaves, and the thick branches created a private world in which we talked. Here on the mountain we seemed to be able to see each other more clearly than before and to talk more freely.

Later, Ruth and I were sitting in the living room after lunch on Sunday as she reminisced about her childhood and the early years of her marriage. It was a beautiful room with its hand-hewn log walls, the flowers and greenery from her garden which Ruth had arranged, the view of the mist-covered valley below. We were in front of the fire. It started raining and we needed the fire to take the damp chill off the room. Ruth apologized for the rain, but when I told her that I had always liked the sound of the rain and the feel of it on my face, she smiled and said, "I always associate rain with happy times. When I was little, we would read and play games on rainy days."

I thought of how much Ruth loved this house where her children had grown up and of all the beauty she had created in it. I realized that Ruth was still making adjustments in her marriage and that even now she was learning to accept her husband's reluctance to live the quiet round-the-hearth retirement life that she perhaps once thought possible. A lifetime of travel, a constant succession of new faces and places, had made it difficult for Billy Graham to settle down peacefully.

(from *Special People*)

The Dream Home

Franklin Graham

*W*hen my folks acquired the property, there were some abandoned buildings on the land but no house. So Mother began planning her dream home. Mama is a free, independent spirit who is not afraid to cut her own path. Also, as a result of growing up in a missionary family in China, she is extremely practical and always eager to make do with what's available. So she decided to build a roomy, old-fashioned log home to house our large family.

Although log homes are popular again in certain areas of the country, in the 1950s most people who had a choice didn't live in a log cabin! But this is what Mama wanted, so she searched the Blue Ridge Mountains for old logs and ended up buying three abandoned cabins—at a very good price, I'm sure. These cabins (some were over two hundred years old) were dismantled and the logs brought to Little Piney Cove.

There, with her plans in hand and a team of mountain craftsmen, she built our home. Mama always found projects like this to work on while Daddy was away preaching. I'm sure this helped pass the time and eased the loneliness she felt.

When construction of our log home got underway, Mama drove up the rocky mountain road just about every day to supervise. I loved tagging along to watch. From as far back as I can remember, I have loved the outdoors, so the excitement of a construction site in a rugged setting like Little Piney Cove was about as good as it got for a boy like me.

(from *Rebel with a Cause*)

SIMPLE MOUNTAIN FURNITURE
BETTY FRIST

The house is furnished with simple mountain pieces that Ruth picked up here and there through the mountains. A friend laughs and says that some of the people who sold her the furniture felt they should have paid her rather than charged her to take it off their hands.

At first, Billy felt the same way. He found it difficult to welcome with open arms some of Ruth's "as is" choices. One day in a friend's home, he pointed to a sorry-looking antique that was in line for refinishing and said, "That's the kind that Ruth likes."

Because of his attitude, whenever Ruth would buy an antique, she'd put it in her car trunk and say jokingly to a friend (whose husband felt the same way Billy did), "If Billy sees it first, it's yours. If your husband sees it first, it's mine."

Well aware of the difference of opinion between them, a friend produced a cartoon which was guaranteed to make both of them laugh. It pictured a crowd gathered at an antique auction. The auctioneer was holding up an antique and saying, "Sold to the woman with her husband's hand over her mouth."

Ruth's mother also took a dim view of some of Ruth's purchases. After seeing her pay cash on the barrelhead for several battered pieces that needed intensive care, she pointed to an old beat-up piece in the dusty antique shop and said, "Ruth, why don't you buy that? It's rotten too."

(from *My Neighbors, the Billy Grahams*)

GRANDMOTHER'S HOUSE

BERDJETTE TCHIVIDJIAN BARKER

I sort of liked the girl things about the house. I liked the warmth of it. I loved the comfort, the grandmother type of things—coming down the stairs in the morning and smelling the eggs and bacon. The little projects she might have you do, like cutting out Christmas cards and pressing flowers.

Also, there was always the mysterious part of the attic that was locked. That was intriguing to us because she told us it was filled with presents for Christmas and we weren't allowed to go in. I've been in since, but there is still mystery there.

The Graham home in winter.

I was a true believer in Santa Claus. We were sitting around Christmas Eve. It was getting late and we heard some bells ring. And she was like, "Oh, Santa Claus is landing on the roof, you better get to bed." I remember the fear that if I didn't get to bed I wouldn't get presents, and I just took off upstairs to bed. I went to sleep just sure he had arrived. The next morning we were opening Christmas presents and we heard those bells again and I heard Ned say, "Oh, Mom, I forgot to take the bells down." That was the last I believed in Santa Claus.

There was always a sense of excitement at Christmas. She especially played it up. On Christmas morning everyone could go into the kitchen but you couldn't go through the swinging door into the living room until it was time. Then she opened the door and we could go in. I just remembered we were always waiting.

I love her practicality. Again, maybe those are things I relate to, and I like to see that some traits I have come from her. To me it's an honor to have any little bits of her character. She hasn't had to have a lot to do a lot. She likes to shop, but she's very frugal and creative. She makes do and makes things out of nothing. You see examples of this all over her house. When we were little she used to take her old Christmas cards and she'd cut out the little pictures and tell us, "Now you can use these little pictures for cards and ornaments next year or put them on packages as tags. We know she has the means to go buy tags for her packages but she get a thrill out of the creative use of things. It has something to do with growing up in China where things just didn't become trash. They used everything.

The Packrat

Maurie Scobie

*R*uth is the classic packrat. She told me that early on from her comings and goings with the Graham family. Probably her upbringing, the fact she was separated from her family to go to school so far away, caused her to treasure things. Every little thing would have been something to hold onto. She did save everything.

She told me she had all these hodge-podge collections of things she had saved from when they were in college. In between doing stuff for the office, Mr. Graham, and the crusade travels, whenever he happened to be out of town on a non-crusade trip, maybe a speaking engagement, then Ruth would holler and say let's do this, that, and the other.

One of the first things we did was put up shelving in one of the attics and then went to an office supply place and found some protective boxes and we started filing material. There was a box titled "College" and "Marriage" and then one for each year after. Then we just started emptying drawers and filing cabinets, suitcases, briefcases, boxes, and put them in chronological order. At some point Mr. G came upstairs to the attic to observe the situation and he felt it was unnecessary to save everything.

Playfully, he would, at intervals over the next few years, say, in front of Ruth, "Darlin', I've asked Maurie to get an eighteen-wheeler up here tomorrow, and he is emptying that attic. We're throwing everything away." And she would always have a playful response to him.

It wasn't until the Cove had opened and they hired someone with experience in museum displays that everything from the attic was taken over to the Cove. When Mr. G came through the first time, I bet he thanked me a half-dozen times. He just didn't see the need in keeping these things, but when he saw how beautifully they came together shelf by shelf, display by display, he saw there was a wealth of value in the stuff from the attic.

A SIMPLE, NICE HOME

I've had the great privilege of going to the Grahams' home. The thing that impressed me the most was the simple way they live. They are true Christians. We've had so many bad examples of what it is to be a Christian, but to me, their lives are the purest form of how you should live your life. They have devoted their lives to everyone to be able to spread joy and love through their belief in their faith. They live very simply and humbly. They have good taste, but it's not expensive. It's just simple and nice. There's a purity about them. I was impressed with that, and I don't know how many people realize that. I think it is important for people to know just what wonderful people they are. It's that simple.

—ANDIE MACDOWELL

A "Do-It-Yourself" Decorator

Every room in the house has Ruth's unique imprint and is breathtakingly charming. Any one of the rooms would be perfectly at home gracing the cover of the slick decorator magazines, and it isn't necessary that a person have the key to Fort Knox to open the door to these rooms. Ruth has proven that a room can have a mouthwatering effect without being overly expensive.

As a "do-it-yourself" decorator, Ruth refuses to be poured into a mold. She does exactly what she wants to do. Sometimes she displays elegant silver in an old pine cupboard. Sometimes the curtains against the living-room log walls are Early American, yellow-and-white-checked gingham, but at times she startles your eye by putting sheer embroidered curtains against the rough walls. If she finds a color she likes in a satin material, she'll turn it wrong side out and use the dull backside for slipcovers or pillows.

—BETTY FRIST, *My Neighbors, the Billy Grahams*

A Comfortable Life

Neither Mother nor Daddy has ever been materialistic. Daddy doesn't care at all about material things. He'd just as soon have one sweater or one suit.

They were very careful in the way they furnished their home, the way they built their home, and people of all walks of life that have come through our home have felt comfortable there.

It's been a comfortable life, but it hasn't been extravagant.

If you go in some people's homes you see photos of the rich and famous signed and framed and on display for visitors to see. But not at Little Piney Cove. The photos are around various rooms, and they're treasured, but not really put out to impress people.

There are five fireplaces in the home. Daddy told Mother she could have one fireplace. But when Daddy went to India, Mother told the builder, "You build fireplaces faster than you ever have in your life." This might not sound very spiritual but Mother taught us that we should always look for a man to marry we were willing to adjust to, but when it came to submitting, "There's a time to quit submitting and start outwitting." So she outwitted Daddy with the five fireplaces and she's got her five fireplaces.

—GIGI GRAHAM TCHIVIDJIAN

FLOWERS, BIRDS, BATS, AND SNAKES

*H*as anyone mentioned her love of flowers at the house? The window boxes and the yard are profuse with color. That was a big project every spring—to get the flowers planted in the beds, the window boxes, and the wheelbarrow by the door. She loves the flowers. And the birds too. She has bird feeders everywhere. She loved the wildlife on the mountain. And bats, and snakes.

—EVELYN FREELAND

Flowers

Most of the time the house inside and out is a welter of flowers—a veritable flower basket. Large geraniums were Ruth's specialty, but since the wilderness is closing in on them, she has replaced geraniums with begonias and impatiens. Her flower boxes are something to behold. The variegated flowers in them strut in their flamboyantly colored plumage in a blaze of glory against the tannish gray log walls.

—BETTY FRIST, *My Neighbors, the Billy Grahams*

The Annual Planting of the Flowers

I moved up here in February twenty-six years ago, and the annual planting of the flowers was my first big project. Growing up in East Texas, my mother didn't plant flowers. Even on my first two or three trips to Montreat, Ruth was always buying flowers, making arrangements. I realized flowers were a big part of her life.

Typically, sometime in March or April, Ruth would start just driving around. Every year would have been different color schemes or types of flowers, where to plant them, how to plant them. It's always a lot of fun. She's pretty much a decisive person, so it's not like she changes her mind after the flowers are planted. I never saw her draw it out, so it must have just been in her head. We always added, but rarely took anything away. It would be like an artist painting a picture. It just seemed like every two or three days she'd be jumping in the car and always came back full of flowers. We're talking hundreds of flowers.

—MAURIE SCOBIE

Caring for the Birds

Ruth is very caring about the birds, and all winter long we've got to make sure that we have enough birdseed because they love the birds both coming and going. There was a night when we were running low and she got me on the two-way, and I called back to the house. Mr. Graham answered and relayed to Ruth, "Darlin', Maurie's on the phone. What are you wanting him for?" She said, "Would he stop and bring up a bag of wild birdseed?" Mr. Graham then said, "She's wants wild birdseed, but I could care less. Tame birdseed would be better." He's funnier than most people think.

—MAURIE SCOBIE

The Skewer

Ruth is known for killing snakes. She had this long skewer she'd cook marshmallows on (it looked like some torture tool you would find in the Tower of London), and she'd go out and stab it with the fork.

The very first time I interviewed Ruth for my biography of her (which started out as a newspaper story in 1979), she was sitting on the couch in her living room and she was hooked up on the mike and we were talking about something. All of a sudden she got up, unplugged the tape recorder, grabbed the marshmallow fork off the hearth, went over to the grandfather clock, and started stabbing under it. I didn't know what was going on and thought maybe I had asked the wrong question. There was a mouse and she finally got the mouse on the fork, stuck it out the door, and fed it to the Doberman pincer. (And she wonders why I started writing about violence when I finished her biography.) I was rather traumatized. One could go on and on with similar anecdotes. There's just not anybody like her.

—PATRICIA CORNWELL

Favorite Times of Year

*B*ecause I think of Mother as being introspective I would think fall and winter were her favorite times of year. I think that's when she would come into herself. When we were children she gave spring and summer over to us. But in fall and winter she was coming into herself more and more, thinking and reflecting. She loves snowstorms. She loves rain. She *loves* a rainy day and a great big thunderstorm. She loves to walk in the fall leaves and have them crunch under her feet.

—GIGI GRAHAM TCHIVIDJIAN

Snowstorms

Every time we get a snowstorm, I immediately think of her. And I think of her up at the house just loving it, sitting by her window with a big smile on her face. I know she loves it and thinks it's beautiful.

—BERDJETTE TCHIVIDJIAN BARKER

Getting Snowed In

She loves it when she gets snowed in the house by herself with a good book. She loves her home. To be alone after the children were gone and to be alone when he was away was never a problem. She always had a fire going, in the kitchen, the living room, or her bedroom, or all three. I think the fellas have carried an awful lot of wood up there.

With a lot of women, being at home alone would cause some fear. But with Ruth, she's enjoyed the quiet, reading, praying, making phone calls, writing, studying.

—MAURIE SCOBIE

Chapter Eight

OTHERS

Those who bring sunshine to the life of others cannot keep it from themselves.

—JAMES M. BARRIE

SHE BRINGS OUT THE BEST IN PEOPLE

EVELYN FREELAND

When I first came to work for Ruth I had no precon-
ceived idea about her, because I don't think we, as a
public, knew that much about her. She was quietly at home raising
her kids.

But she had a tremendous, unheralded ministry with people in
the community who were hurting—taking care of people's difficulties. Always taking meals to people who had some situation, like a
death or serious illness. She cared for others and if she wasn't able to
do it herself, she had those who were helping her do it, like taking
food to people.

She taught a Sunday school class in Montreat in the late 60s and
also a Bible class on the names of God for some of the women in
the community. I went to a couple of those.

She still hears from students from that Sunday school class. One
of them dropped by recently and just stuck his head in the door to
say hello. They are all people who are grown and have grandkids.

I was aware of her interest in the college students and often she
had groups of them up to the house. Her home was open to students particularly when Mr. Graham was away. She very much set
aside her own agenda when he came home so that she could spend
time with him and minister in whatever way he wished.

Her example of perseverance in pain, humor, and her genuine
concern for others are the characteristics I see shine in her.

She is the most unforgettable person I've ever met. She's such a
real person. She didn't ask for the kind of life she's been handed. She
had no idea what the future was going to be. Whatever has come her
way, she has faced with grace and with love and with caring. She's

just a very real person. She's comfortable with people in high places, and she's comfortable with somebody on the street. Wherever she happens to be, she's just herself. She's not trying to be anything she's not, at any time.

She made it very comfortable for me to work with her, because I could also be myself. Not everyone is comfortable enough to make fun of themselves. She brings out the best of those who are around her.

I'm a quiet, not totally self-confident, person but around Ruth that's never been a problem. We enjoyed good fellowship and talking through things. I've always enjoyed working with her, even when we were under pressure, working on a book deadline.

THE GRAHAMS ENTERED MY LIFE WHEN
EVERYONE ELSE WALKED OUT

JIM BAKKER

The Grahams entered my life when everyone else walked out.

I first met Billy Graham hosting my own program which that week was originating at the National Religious Broadcasters. It was the height of my ministry. There were thousands of people, lights, cameras. The team was there: Cliff Barrows, George Beverly Shea, and others. It was a great moment for me because I had a lot of people I wanted to interview in my life, and Billy Graham was one of them. I remember the first moment I got to interview Dr. Billy Graham. That was a great moment for me.

But I also remember the last time I saw Dr. Graham. I was in prison, very sick, and facing a forty-five-year prison sentence. It was one of my lowest moments. I was incarcerated in Rochester, Minnesota, and I had been assigned the job of cleaning toilets. That day I got up to clean toilets even though I had a fever and the flu. After I cleaned the toilets I had my old clothes on and just laid across the bunk, trying to get warm, putting blankets over me. The guard came and said, "Bakker, come with me." I didn't know where I was going. The guard said, "Don't you have a coat?" I got my coat and thought I was going out to empty the big garbage containers. As an orderly, that was part of my job. So I had on the tennis shoes I wore when cleaning the toilets, with my toes hanging out, and I looked like a man who had been sleeping under a bridge for days. As the guard led me across the compound of the prison, I wondered what I had done wrong and was thinking, *Where is this guard escorting me?*

I'd been to the warden's office but had never had an escort before. I kept thinking, *What is going wrong? What's happening?* I was sick, my hair was a mess. By the time I got to the warden's office, I was a little frightened of what was happening to me.

One of the executives came out of the warden's conference room, and they said, "Bakker." They never use your first name. "You have a visitor; do you want your visit?"

My mind raced. It wasn't visiting day. I said, "What do you mean?" and he said, "Didn't anybody tell you?" I said, "No. No, they didn't tell me."

He said, "Billy Graham is here to see you." And I looked down at my shoes with my toes hanging out, my rumpled clothes. My mind raced back to those days when he sat with me when I was dressed in a nice suit. It was a different day and a different time and I was embarrassed and almost said no. But I thought, *He's come to see me, so I better do it because only Billy Graham and the president of the United States can walk into a federal prison when they want to see somebody.*

So I walked into the warden's office and there was Dr. Graham standing bigger than life with his arms outstretched. I walked into his arms and he hugged me and said, "Jim, I love you."

The thing I remember the most is that he talked to me as a human being. In prison you are talked to like an animal. And he gave me dignity.

Franklin came to see me often after that and spoke to all the prisoners. Franklin Graham is the kind of man Proverbs speaks about in chapter 17, verse 17: "A friend loves at all times, and a brother is born for adversity" [NIV]. So Franklin kept coming.

When I got near the end of my prison sentence, I needed a sponsor to get out. I needed someone to give me a job and guarantee me a place to live. And the Christmas before I was scheduled to get out, Franklin came and said, "Jim, I want to be your sponsor. I want to help you get out of prison." I thought about that and told him, "You can't do it. You don't need the scandal that's connected to me. You don't need my baggage. I've got a lot of press and a lot of problems, and the Graham name doesn't need that." Franklin looked at me and said, "Jim Bakker, you were my friend before. You helped me build that hospital in Africa when no one else wanted to help me. You were my friend then, and you're my friend now. If anyone doesn't like it, I'm looking for a fight."

I found out later that Ruth Graham was the player behind the scenes. She was the one who encouraged Billy to visit. She was that silent, powerful woman behind the scenes.

When I was released from prison I was assigned to Asheville to live and work with the Salvation Army. Coming out of prison I was frightened and had the idea that people were going to spit on me. But within forty-eight hours of my arrival at the Salvation Army, Ruth Graham called the Salvation Army and asked if they would allow me to be her guest at church on Sunday morning. When they came and told me, I could not believe it. I did not think anyone would want to sit with me in church. They gave permission, so on Sunday I was driven to the church, where the pastor welcomed me and met with me in his office. And then he escorted me out into the church. Franklin was preaching that night, and there were two seats left in that entire church. It was packed. They seated me and the organ started playing. It was quiet and then the doors opened in the back. In walked Ruth Graham and she walked down the aisle and sat down next to me. Without saying a word she told the whole world, "Jim Bakker is my friend." I was so wounded and so frightened, but this great woman thought to reach out to me to help me move back into life.

That day, after lunch at her house, Ruth asked me for an address, and I pulled out an envelope (because they don't let you have a wallet in prison). She said, "Don't you have a wallet?" And I said, "This is my wallet." She said, "That's an envelope," and left the room and came back with a wallet. She said, "Here, this is one of Billy's wallets. He doesn't need this, it's an extra one." I still have that wallet to this day.

I'll never forget her, and I wish I could thank her for the healing she began in my heart.

HELPING OTHERS
BETTY FRIST

*O*ne day a visitor went to the Graham home and found Ruth in the kitchen, cradling a strange baby in one arm, fixing breakfast with her free hand, and trying to shut the oven door with her foot. The baby's parents were young missionaries home on furlough and were desperate for sleep because of the travel-worn, upset baby. So Ruth had taken the baby into her room for an all-night stand while the parents caught up on their sleep.

A friend reports that one summer she opened her home in Montreat to find that Ruth and her mother had bought material for curtains for the entire house, made them, and hung them on rods which they'd also bought and installed. As an added bonus, Ruth had found out the approximate time of her arrival and had gone back to turn on the electric blanket.

One Montreat resident tells that when she and her son came down with the flu, Ruth and the children came down the mountain to their home. While the patients were feebly protesting, Ruth pulled them bodily out of bed and took them home, where they were given intensive care and cheerful round-the-clock room service until they were on foot again. She adds, "Ruth could have used the excuse that she also had Billy in bed with the flu, but that would never have occurred to her."

Ruth is also thoughtful in the so-called "little areas," though that is a misnomer. Sometimes these areas give an even clearer insight into a person's character. A visitor in the Graham home tells of mentioning a certain book that she was interested in reading—then of leaving and going to a nearby tearoom to have lunch with friends. She says, "I'd forgotten all about the book when I looked up and saw Ruth, a vision in yellow wool, coming through the door of the tearoom with the book in her hand." Although she was scheduled to meet Billy's plane arriving from Europe, she'd clocked the time she had left, then gone through the maze of books in the home until she'd put her hand on the one in question.

(from *My Neighbors, the Billy Grahams*)

A Favorite Character in Town

Patricia Cornwell

The first time Ruth and I met was when I was nine years old. It was Christmas and I was in fourth grade. My mother tried to bring her three kids up here in the snow because she was very depressed and my father left the family. We'd been snowed in and out of school for weeks and were short of groceries, fuel oil, and our car was stranded down at the gate hill, so my mom was walking her three little kids up this snowy mountain road. I still remember the caretaker, Mr. Rickman, in his orange Jeep with his snowplow on the front. He asked my mom, "What are you doing? Where are you going?" because she looked a little odd walking these kids up the mountain. She said, "We're going up to see the Grahams, and they're expecting us." Of course, Ruth wasn't expecting us; she didn't even know us. But this is a typical story of how Ruth has always taken care of other people, which is something special most people don't know about.

So we rode up the mountain in that Jeep and I still remember sitting in the back on that metal floor, I could smell the spare tire and had no idea where we were going. I was excited because it seemed like we were going on some sort of adventure. Then we arrived at the house, this beautiful log house with the snow everywhere, the smoke curling out of the chimney and Ruth standing in the open doorway with this long skirt on and a shawl wrapped around her with her hair up in a French twist. Ruth was the most beautiful, warm person I'd ever seen. It was like something out of a fairy tale.

Even though she did not know us, she invited us in to lunch. There was a great big fire in her living room. She had fixed spaghetti for lunch and had written her son, Ned's, name with a noodle on a plate. I remember that clearly.

My mother gave Ruth a note trying to give her kids to Ruth to take care of us. My mother was very depressed. That's what is known as a Trojan horse and when it rolls up in your yard you should send it back.

That was my very first contact I had with Ruth and it seems such a strange story that that nine-year-old little girl would later become her biographer.

Everybody in Montreat knew two things about Ruth Bell Graham. First, she was a poet and a real artist. You can drive up to her house and see cartoon figures she has drawn on shutters as well as other signs of Ruth's creativity and very quirky sense of humor. Second, you didn't want to be on the road when she was driving. She'd be in this little blue VW Carmengia and you could hear her coming. Vrooom. If I was on my bicycle I was always told to get off the road. She'd come flying around these curves. She got her fair share of speeding tickets.

She was a favorite character in town. Everybody was always telling the latest story about what she had done. For example, one neighbor had just lost her husband, and Ruth called her up and said, "I'd like to bring your family Sunday dinner."

She made pot roast, but the family was going to Sunday school so the neighbor had told her just to set the roast in the oven. Well, while Ruth was there, she noticed the oven was dirty, so she cleaned the oven. About a week later Ruth was sitting behind this person in church and finally the woman couldn't stand it any longer and turned around in the middle of the sermon and said, "Did you clean my oven?"

RELIGION IN SHOE LEATHER
CALVIN THIELMANN

Ruth is the most unforgettable character I've ever met, easily. She's remarkable, spontaneous, and loves people. She loves to help people. She's a "doer of the Word and not a hearer only." She's like the Book of James, religion in shoe leather. She goes and does what everyone talks about.

For instance, she helped pay to bury a poor mountain man who died in a nearby hospital, and I could tell you a hundred stories like that. One of the most unforgettable pictures I have of Ruth was when we went to Asheville with Dennis Agajanian, a preacher and musician. While we were in Asheville, one of the guys went into one of those adult bookstores and yelled at the people in there, "You're going to go to hell if you don't get out of this place." A policeman came running and was going to arrest Ruth. I got in a row with the cop, and he said we needed to get a permit. So we did get a permit and held an open-air service in front of the bookstore. On that same trip we went by the jail, I guess to get our permit, so we decided we would preach to the people in the jail. I can remember Dennis singing "Amazing Grace." That hymn always touches people because everyone seems to know it. There was some ragged, dirty lady who was definitely at a low point in her life and she started to cry. Tears came running down her face, and Ruth reached through the bars and held her hand all through the song. I wanted a picture of that scene because it was just like Ruth.

WENDY'S STORY
JULIE NIXON EISENHOWER

*S*he told another story, a moving one about meeting a young girl named Wendy during a month-long crusade in London. Wendy, a heavy drug user, came to the crusade night after night, but she was still not committed, still searching. Wendy and Ruth had many talks together. One evening before the service began, Ruth told the girl, "One day you will come to something difficult in your life. And then you will either go back on drugs or go on with Christ."

A few days before the end of the crusade, Ruth was sitting in the stadium at Earls Court when someone passed her a note from Wendy. "I am on drugs," she read. "Come help me." When Ruth found Wendy by the stadium entrance, she was almost unconscious. A girl with her explained that Wendy's best friend had died from an overdose that afternoon. Ruth took a package of Kleenex from her handbag, the only paper she could find, and on its cardboard backing she quickly wrote:

> God loves me.
> Jesus died for me.
> No matter what I've done, if I confess to Him, He will forgive me.

She tucked the cardboard in Wendy's pocket and then one of the crusade staff members took the girl home. A year later, Ruth met Wendy again in London. Wendy asked Ruth about the note she had found in her pocket. She had no recollection whatsoever of having asked Ruth for help, but that message Ruth had left with her had been her lifeline to God, she said.

Ruth believes with all her heart in that simple message she gave Wendy. The act of confession and acceptance of God's love means that no man need suffer the cruel fate of hell. And hell is very real to Ruth. She describes it as "eternal separation from God."

(from *Special People*)

COMPLETE ACCEPTANCE OF OTHERS

*T*he overwhelming experience one has when you are with the Grahams is their complete openness, friendliness, and acceptance. You're in their presence twenty seconds and it feels you've been there a lifetime. There is no barrier between them and the people with whom they share space. Ruth's presence just makes people light up. She's a tremendously talented person in sharing joy.

—DR. OLSON HUFF

Esteeming Others

"Each esteeming others as greater than themselves." This is how they've treated those who surround them and each other. And they do it all with "a peace that passeth understanding." They have an unbelievable memory for people—and they love them.

—KARLENE SHEA

Helping the Underdog

I love the way she would reach out to the people around Montreat. Ruth has always had a thing for the underdog—the person who was on the outside, always reaching out to them, helping them in every way she possibly could. And even if they believed or not, she was their friend.

—LEIGHTON FORD

An Enormous Capacity for Others

Both of them are very gracious people in the sense that they are not caught up in themselves. They're very interested in others, with a heart that beats for God but also with an enormous capacity for other people and to love the world at large.

—ANNE GRAHAM LOTZ

Billy's Bibles

Ruth helped me to get Bibles for prisoners. We called it smuggling in, but we really are allowed to get them in. Once she sent me a couple of cases and she wrote, "These are Billy's Bibles. I went to his library and saw he had so many different Bibles that he didn't need them all." So now, unbeknownst to them, prisoners all over the world have Billy's Bibles.

—JIM BAKKER

Lobbying with Politicians

At a dinner in the White House, in 1973 during the visit when Ruth and I had our private talk, she asked my father if there was any way of sending Bibles to all the Americans in foreign prisons. She was especially concerned by news stories about young men and women in foreign hell-holes on drug charges. As a result of her request, the State Department provided the information needed so that the Billy Graham Evangelistic Association could send Bibles to prisons around the world. They are sent in the hope that somehow the Bibles will be delivered to all the prisoners once they arrive.

I realize there are many people who feel that he was not neutral in his relationship with my father during his presidency. But the close friendship between our families, which dates from 1950, the year my father was elected to the Senate, made a more "correct" distance virtually impossible. It was largely due to my grandmother, Hannah Nixon, that our families became friends. Nana met Billy Graham in 1947 when he was an unknown minister with Youth of Christ. She remembered him, and two years later attended the Los Angeles Crusade, which was his first major evangelical effort. A year or so later, my father and Billy were introduced in the Senate dining room by a Democratic senator. My grandmother was the chief subject of their first brief conversation.

—JULIE NIXON EISENHOWER, *Special People*

Under the Radar

Because of Mr. Graham's travels and because Ruth is such an incredibly gifted, talented, and creative person, she's just got her hands in all kinds of things. Mr. G had me help on his major trips, but when I came back home I would be up at the house all the time just helping Ruth do everything she was into with family, friends, and the community. Ruth has always been a real quiet, behind-the-scenes person, just loving and helping everyone in the community. She would rely on staff and church friends and her pastor to make her aware of certain hardships with certain families, then someone like me (and other staff members) could quietly carry out helping financially, paying a bill, taking them food, or tiptoeing into their kitchen and washing the dishes. There is a lot they do quietly that a lot of people just don't even know about.

—MAURIE SCOBIE

No Condemnation

One word that does not apply to Mother in any form is condemnation. She has a marvelous capacity to accept people where and as they are. As someone has written of another, it applies to Mother: "She did not try to set others right; she only listened to and loved and understood her fellow-creatures." However, she does have difficulty with those who attack the ones she loves. She is fiercely loyal. She stays in touch with an assortment of friends—from a London waif she has tried to nurture along, to those of royal blood, to the mountain men who helped build our house, to early childhood friends.

—RUTH GRAHAM MCINTYRE

A Sensitive Child

Always as a child she was sensitive, much more so than I. I think that's a good trait, but it can also be a burden because you feel other people's hurts and suffer with them. If you weren't that sensitive you could just put on a raincoat and go on your way.

—ROSA BELL MONTGOMERY

A Positive Person

She's a very positive person. I don't think I've ever been around her and left thinking she was depressed or down. She's just always positive. She sees the positive in everything, people too. She accepts you where you are. She may see that a person needs to mature or grow, but she encourages you where you are. I don't feel like she ever judges people. They may be doing things she disagrees with or living ways she does not agree with biblically, but she will never judge them; she just continues to love them.

I was having a hard time with one of my boys once and felt really discouraged. And I didn't think I was being a good mom. She just piped up, "No, no. You're doing a great job; you're a great mom." Her little comments built me up tremendously. And I know she doesn't do that with just me. She does that with everyone with whom she comes into contact.

She just has a confidence about her. She's very comfortable with herself. Some confident people can be focused on themselves, but she's not.

—BERDJETTE TCHIVIDJIAN BARKER

You Can Judge Someone by How They Treat People

The thing that's also so precious about Ruth is that she cares so much about individuals. She cares so much about people. You can judge someone by how they treat people who aren't important. That's the true measure of a human being.

When I was growing up, I saw that firsthand. Ruth always cared about us common folk that lived down the hill, no matter who it was—one of the neighborhood kids, or someone who was sick or had a need. She has never acted like she was better than other people.

—Patricia Cornwell

Touched by Ruth

There's a constant demand for her time, not only from her family, but also other people. Anyone who gets to know Ruth wants to spend more time with her. When you're with her you sit up straighter, you have your best smile, and you think higher thoughts. Ruth inspires one.

She has some tiles in her kitchen of a shepherdess. You always think of a shepherd as being a man or a boy but in some countries you will see a picture of a shepherdess. I think of her as shepherding, not only her children and her husband, but the community in a way. She was very influential at the college for a long time and for various students. She likes to help someone who's in trouble. She couldn't go to Tibet, so she endeavored to help people by her written word and by love and action behind the scenes. One boy was a rebel. He was floundering like a little ship out to sea. Someone introduced her to him and she had him come up to the house and she gave him some work to do. It gave him confidence in himself. The next time I saw him he was sitting up straighter. He had some goals and he was a different person. Ruth had touched him. It happened over and over again.

—Karlene Shea

Chapter Nine

HUMOR

A sense of humor keen enough to show a man his own absurdities, as well as those of other people, will keep him from the commission of all sins, or nearly all, save those that are work committing.

—Samuel Butler, *Lord, What Is Man?*

AN INTERESTING MIXTURE OF DEEP SPIRITUALITY AND MISCHIEVOUS FUN
BETTY FRIST

Ruth said that every date with Billy at Wheaton College turned out to be either a preaching or religious service of some kind. Yet she found, under all his dedication and depth, an irresistible winsomeness. Ruth also recognized the fact that not only was Billy older in chronological age than the other students, he was already a mature person in other ways, having his sights set on definite goals and a determination not to be sidetracked.

To balance this seriousness, God gave Billy a wife who wouldn't seem out of place in a stained glass window, yet who has enough humor to "prop him up on his leanin' side" when burdens become so great one wonders if the gaiety can ever survive the gloom. When Billy arrives home, pressured as few men have been pressured, Ruth takes her fun seriously, feeling that there are some things "too important to be serious about." I'm reminded of what Ruth's father said of her childhood: "An interesting mixture of deep spirituality and mischievous fun." Christianity has never lobbied against wholesome laughter; the Bible says there is "a time to weep and a time to laugh" (Ecclesiastes 3:4) and "A merry heart doeth good like a medicine" (Proverbs 17:22).

For example: On one occasion, Ruth had several women friends to dinner. Among them was an older friend who had dangerously high blood pressure plus a serious heart condition, and her doctor had taken her off desserts. However, she kept insisting that Ruth give her a piece of blueberry pie along with everyone else. Ruth felt it would be tantamount to holding a loaded gun at her head, and she refused to serve her. The friend persisted, so Ruth finally left the table and in a few minutes was back with a hefty slice of pie, plus a mountain of whipped cream topping which the other guests didn't have. The guest started eating it, then looked quizzically at Ruth and put her fork down. The whipped cream had come out of Billy's pressurized shaving cream can.

Ruth is a neighborly sort of person and likes to share food, or whatever, so one of her neighbors was looking forward with anticipation to a tasty meal when she was handed a sack labeled, "Meat for your supper," which Ruth had sent down by a workman on the place. When she opened it up, a long, black, groggy snake slithered out. Ruth later said she thought she'd killed it; she'd only stunned it. Snakes abound in the area. Although, at the time, the Grahams had lived there only a few years, the man who worked on the place told me he'd already killed ninety-five rattlers. On one occasion, Ruth and a companion met a rattler face to face on the mountain. Ruth hit it with a large rock, then got in the Jeep and ran over it with the wheels. But it took the addition of a wrench to kill it. She insisted that she didn't know whether she'd killed it or if it had died of a coronary from fright at hearing the companion scream.

One night T. W. Wilson, a staff member with the Billy Graham Evangelistic Association, called Ruth and in great excitement told her to rush to the yard and see a UFO in the sky near the mountain ridge. Ruth called Ned, who was the only one at home, and they hurried outside but could find nothing. Then Ruth realized it was the first of April. Unwilling to be bested by T. W., she told Ned to stay in the background and scream like a banshee while she called T. W. Getting him on the phone while Ned was furnishing the backdrop of screaming, Ruth shouted into the telephone, "It's landing in our yard!" and slammed down the receiver. Then she and Ned went out to sit on the steps and listen to T. W.'s car tires squealing as his car careened around the mountain curves hurling up the mountain, and braking to a sudden stop in the driveway. Ruth said sweetly, "April Fool" to T. W. and a companion he had with him. T. W. was incensed. He told Ruth that not only had he and his companion seen the UFO, but that several neighbors had also witnessed it. Finally, even Ruth was convinced they'd seen some strange object, but T. W. was still a little miffed. As he started home he said to Ruth from the car window, "Even if one should land in your yard, don't call me."

For a good many years in Montreat, lot lines were often scrambled, with one owner not knowing where her line stopped and another's started. A friend of Ruth's had bought a lot and, though planning to build, wasn't quite ready to start. She was reduced to a severe case of nerves when she received a letter from Ruth, an excerpt of which follows: "Just a hurried note in case you haven't already heard. They're building on your property. I'm positive they haven't gotten permission, but they're notorious for that sort of thing. Do you want me to do anything about it?" (By this time the friend was a candidate for the hospital emergency room.) On the next page Ruth wrote, "I'm not sure what they are—swallows or phoebes. But the nest is above your back living-room window."

Ruth's fun reaches all the way back to boarding-school days in Korea when she and a friend pulverized mothballs and poured the resulting mess into the salt shakers on the table. Obviously, the spaghetti lunch ended in the garbage cans. In looking back on the incident now, she regrets the waste of food.

(from My Neighbors, the Billy Grahams)

"She'll Be Coming 'Round the Mountain When She Comes"

Maurie Scobie

This story has appeared in Ruth's book *Footprints of a Pilgrim*, but I was there and my perspective was a little different. Of course, after the wreck we weren't going to say anything about it because it was a brand-new Volvo and it was a little bit embarrassing. But later, after it happened, the police said this was a typical thing that happened to someone in their seventies or eighties, when they accidentally hit the gas instead of the brake.

In most cases it would be to knock down a garbage can, smash the garage, a mailbox, a neighbor's bush. But when you live on the side of the mountain and make that decision, you're airborne for seventy-five yards and demolish your automobile.

Ruth had called earlier that day about her friend Petie from North Korea days. Her son had been killed in a car wreck, and she had come back from the funeral the night before and called Ruth upset about the death of her son. Ruth said, "I'll come and pick you up this afternoon. Come up and spend the evening; we'll have Chinese and I'll take you back home."

I was out doing errands when on the two-way radio I heard Ruth calling someone, saying, "I've run off the road, and I think you are going to need a tow truck." And I thought, *She knows that road backward and forward. And she's driven every vehicle from Jeeps to convertibles to trucks. No way could she run off the road.* After they completed their transmission, I was just coming through the Montreat gate. So I got on the two-way and said, "Hey Ruth, I'll be up there in five minutes; is there anything I can do to help you?" She said, "Well, you better get up here pretty quick," and that's when I sensed something was not right. As I came through their gate, I looked up the side of the mountain and she was about seventy yards straight up the cliff from the house and the car was on its side with the lights on. I said, "Oh my goodness, Ruth, I can see you. Are you really OK?" All she said was, "You better get here quick."

It probably would have been easier to hike up, but I chose to drive all the way to the top of the hill and then hiked down and approached the car. It was only resting on a three-inch tree—the whole weight of the car and it was completely sideways. All I could see were her two hands holding on the steering wheel. I yelled, "Ruth, I'm about six or seven feet from the car. I'm afraid if I get closer it will loosen the tree roots and the car will roll on over. I'm a little nervous, so can you wait a few minutes until someone gets here to help?" She calmly replied, "I think my back's broken, as well as both of my legs with the bone coming through the skin. Blood is dripping everywhere, but if you insist on waiting another five or ten minutes I think I can hold on."

I'm sure I was white in the face. My legs were so weak I could hardly stand. Then I saw Ruth's friend Petie. I saw her hand come around with her thumb pointing down, and she leaned around and she was frowning and shaking her head. And I said, "Ruth, Petie's giving me the indication that this is all a bunch of baloney. Are you trying to give me a heart attack or what?" Then of course she just gave out a big laugh. She just loves to laugh. So sure enough they were OK. David arrived, and he felt it had settled enough. But I don't know if you've ever tried to open a car door on its side. It was all he and I could do to get the door open. I stood in the crack of the door so it wouldn't close. I took her right hand with my two hands and David took her left hand and we pulled Ruth out. Neither one of them had their seat belts on. The tow truck had not arrived yet, but I was so shaken that I told David, "I don't know how we are going to get Ruth and her friend up to the house, but there's no way I can do anything to help you. Can we wait till the tow truck gets here?" Ruth said, "Nothing doing. I'm just going to scoot on my rear end all the way down." So that's what she did, all the way down the hill. Then I asked, by two-way, if someone could come up from the office, and they met us down at the gate and drove us up to the house where we waited for the tow truck.

Because Mr. Graham was gone, I felt the responsibility to make sure everything was all right. So unbeknownst to Ruth I called the police and rescue squad and ask them to come up. Well, she was none too pleased. Sometimes if she did get a little upset she would call me Buster. So she said, "Buster, what do you think you're doing calling these people?" I said, "Mr. Graham would want me to do what I thought was necessary. I knew you wouldn't like it, but I thought the medical team should check you out and make sure you are OK." I don't think they had any cuts or bruises or any aches or pains.

WHAT HAS RUTH SAID THIS TIME?

BETTY FRIST

Even as a child, Ruth showed indelible signs of being the woman she is today. A retired missionary who lived in the same compound with Ruth's family when she was a child, reminiscing, said, "The missionaries used to ask each other, 'Well, what has Ruth done or said this time?'"

Ruth has a notorious inability to be insipid in anything she says or does. When a reporter asked her if Billy ever entertained doubts, she said, "He has them; he doesn't entertain them."

A friend was trying to pick Ruth's brain for a title to an article she was writing on teenagers. In the course of the conversation she said to Ruth, "I'm for teens," and Ruth said, "Then call it Pro-teens."

One day Ruth walked through their living room exuding a heady fragrance. When a guest in the room asked the name of her perfume she said, "Bathroom Spray," and continued to the kitchen.

Ruth is also the perfect example of the nonfrenzy. On one occasion, an agitated teacher sent her a note telling her that her first grader sometimes came to school with wrinkled clothes, like he'd slept in them. Ruth penciled on the note, "They are, and he has," and sent it back to her. He'd gone through a time of being afraid he'd be late to school, so he'd take his bath, then put on clean clothes and sleep in them. Ruth refused to make a killer whale out of a sardine.

One night at dinner in their home, a guest with a bald spot and a quizzical expression kept feeling his head. Then he said, "Ruth, it feels like sawdust is falling on my head." Ruth, unperturbed, said, "It is," without missing a beat in the conversation. She doesn't come unglued over the woodborers who have taken up residence in the massive beams overhead. She said facetiously that she could hear them chewing but also insisted that a shot of insect spray could put them out of commission until the next time. When a guest glances up, he's startled to see a tiny gremlin with an Afro hairdo staring out at him from one of the knotholes in the beam—another evidence of Ruth's droll sense of humor.

One evening Ruth had just finished shampooing her hair and rolling it on curlers when there was a knock at the door. On answering it, she found a VIP and his wife who had arrived for dinner at Billy's invitation—and he'd forgotten to tell her. Ruth didn't make a federal case out of it because emergencies are routine with the Grahams.

It's been said that a person becomes mature when he can laugh at himself. Ruth can.

(from My Neighbors, the Billy Grahams)

JUST A TEASE?

BETTY FRIST

*R*uth, being very attractive, has drawn her share of wolves. Many times during the London Crusade, she'd walk incognito through the crowds in the park, hoping to pick up remarks about the crusade. One day a wolf tried to pick her up. She tried to walk away from him but he followed, so she decided to try to see what made him tick, help him, and invite him to the crusade.

He quickly noted her accent and asked where she was from. She told him, "The United States." He asked, "You aren't by any chance with the crusade, are you?" Ruth answered, "Yes." He was looking a little less ardent but didn't seem to know how to put a period to the conversation. He was tailgating trouble when he asked, "Are you married?" Ruth again replied, "Yes."

"Not to one of the team members?" he asked hopefully, but his face was clearly showing distress signals. Ruth again said, "Yes" and was thoroughly enjoying the look of incredulity gathering on his face. He began to stutter, "Not to . . . not to—?"

"Yes," said Ruth, "to Billy Graham." He dived into the crowd and Ruth continued on, chuckling, but was also concerned that she hadn't been able to help him.

(from *My Neighbors, the Billy Grahams*)

QUICK AND SPONTANEOUS

Ruth is incredibly quick and spontaneous. You can make a remark or pun and Ruth will burst out laughing whereas sometimes Mr. Graham won't quite get it. Of course, to Ruth that can be even more hilarious, when we try to explain just what the humor was in that particular situation or remark.

Occasionally, Ruth would ask me to do something and Mr. Graham would go, "Darlin', don't ask Maurie to do that." I didn't mind. I got a call on the two-way radio one night (before we had cell phones) and was asked to call up to the house. When I called, Mr. Graham answered and said to Ruth, "Honey, this is Maurie. What did you want him to pick up?" She yelled from the other room, "Pink fingernail polish." He said to her, while I was listening, "Darlin', there is no way on earth I'm going to ask Maurie to do that." I said, "Mr. Graham, I heard what she said and I don't mind at all. They're closing soon, so I'll just wiggle on down there now." On the way down there I was thinking, *I hope the place is empty and I can just pick it up quick and go to the counter,* but as it turned out, there were about four women that the Eckerd's clerk was helping. When I reached for the fingernail polish, the women looked at me strange and I said, "Don't worry, I'm not about to parade around Asheville in this. It is for my boss's wife."

—MAURIE SCOBIE

Never Dull

Mother sprinkles all her conversations with humor and understanding. In consequence they are never dull, though sometimes outlandish due to her marvelous sense of the ridiculous. She doesn't take herself so seriously that she cannot laugh at herself. Several years ago she drove up to stay with me for a few days. Having never driven to my home before, she was unsure of the cutoff. But she noticed a little red car with Virginia license tags so she just followed it. By the time she got to Winston-Salem she realized the little red car was not going to Virginia! She had gone hours out of her way. Some would get uptight and frustrated. Not my mother. She was chuckling when she arrived safely—but late—at my home.

—RUTH GRAHAM MCINTYRE

There's Nobody Like Her

Ruth and I have always had an unusual friendship. I've always seen Ruth for who she really is. I've never seen her as an extension of her wonderful husband (who is one of the dearest, sweetest people you would ever meet in your life). Ruth is independent—a real spitfire. There's nobody like her. She's so smart and well read and has a fantastic creativity. I resonate with her wacky sense of humor. I think we have a similar sense of humor. We laugh at a lot of the same things—the absurdity in things. And she's always up for an adventure, whether it's a ride in a helicopter or hang gliding. She's so full of life.

—PATRICIA CORNWELL

Pumpkin Head

This is a ridiculous memory but it stands out as my first conscious memory of my grandmother. We were living in Montreat at the time and I remember her walking down the driveway with a jack-o'-lantern on her head. I guess it was Halloween and she walked down while we were sitting at the table by the large picture window. We saw this person with a big jack-o'-lantern on her head, and since we were young we were a little scared and thought this might be the real thing from Halloween night, but it was my grandmother.

She was the way grandmas were supposed to be despite who she was to the world.

—BERDJETTE TCHIVIDJIAN BARKER

Memories of Joy

I cannot recall what my earliest memory of my mother is, but I am quite certain it is associated with joy. Her joy is all the more notable because her life has not been easy. She has experienced her own stress and hurt and has daily confronted the needs of others from around the world. I now understand that her joy did not stem from perfect or ideal circumstances, but from a deep, abiding faith.

—RUTH ("BUNNY") GRAHAM MCINTYRE

Ruth Is an Imp

We were kids together in China, and Kitty went to college with Ruth. Now we're all living in Montreat.

Ruth is an imp. She loved April Fools Day. We were turned loose on April Fools in that school. We tried to outdo each other with various shenanigans. [Growing up with Ruth] was always fun. Being with Ruth was always an adventure.

She has always been mischievous with a tremendous sense of humor and a great ability to play practical jokes. But she's also kind and generous, and she's been one of the pillars in keeping our China group together.

—GAY CURRIE FOX WITH KITTY PETERSON

Two of a Kind

Barbara Bush was an important part [of George Bush's] quiet self-confidence. A lot of Americans seemed to agree with Ruth's tongue-in-cheek comment that it was worth having George Bush in the White House if only because it made Barbara the First Lady.

She and Ruth were two of a kind in so many ways. No wonder they enjoyed being together. Both of them were totally devoted to their husbands and children. Both of them created a stylish but relaxed home atmosphere, where friends and strangers alike always felt welcome. (When George Bush was Vice President and the Bushes were living in a house on the grounds of the National Observatory, Ruth noticed lots of things Barbara did to transform that musty Victorian mansion into a home.) Both of them had a streak of good-humored impulsiveness that added a note of fun and spontaneity to almost any occasion. And both of them were quick with the quip, especially where their husbands were concerned. (When Ruth answered the phone at our house one day, the caller asked, "Is Billy handy?" "Not very," she retorted, "but he keeps trying!")

Ruth recalls with particular delight one visit we made to the Bushes at their summer home in Kennebunkport, Maine. Upon our arrival, Ruth was told to go to Barbara's bedroom, only to find that Barbara and the neighbors had pushed the bed against the wall, had piled the furniture on top of it to clear an open space, and were all on the floor vigorously exercising in time with a television workout program. Ruth's back problems forced her to sit on the sidelines, but she was sure she had more fun watching than they did exercising.

—BILLY GRAHAM, *Just As I Am*

Chapter Ten

BOOKS AND CREATIVITY

The artist produces for the liberation of his soul. It is his nature to create as it is the nature of water to run down hill.

—W. SOMERSET MAUGHAM

MOTHER'S WORDS
RUTH GRAHAM MCINTYRE

*L*etters from home became one of the few bright spots [when I was at school]. Mama wrote faithfully, usually sending two or three letters a week. With my first glance at the envelope I could always detect Mama's letters from the others. Her distinctive, back-slanted handwriting was unmistakable, and she always used a broad-tipped pen.

Mama's letters always seemed to arrive when I needed them most. It was like a ten-minute visit to Little Piney Cove. When she shared news, I could picture the log house and almost smell the chicken frying in Bea's pan. But more than anything else, Mama's letters were spiritually encouraging—like those penned by the apostle Paul to the early church. Mama's letters always had a verse, a word of comfort, a spiritual lesson. She always concluded with her love and how proud she was of me. I treasured those letters and read them over and over.

Still, there were times I was miserable. It was unlike me to show my feelings, but for at least the first two months, each night when the lights went out, I lay in my bed, covered my head with a blanket so my roommate wouldn't hear, and cried myself to sleep.

Mother feels deeply and has strong opinions on most things. She has always been a private person, and because of her position does not have the privilege of "spouting off." My older sister, Gigi, says Mother would be in better health now if she had kicked a few shins. Instead, she has written. In the preface to her first book of poetry she wrote, "I wrote because I had to. It was write or develop an ulcer—or forget. I chose to write. At times I wrote for the sheer fun." And the world is richer for it. Her suffering has been the seed for the blossoming of rich, thoughtful poetry, personal accounts of the worldwide ministry of my father, humorous insights, and always a record of her pilgrimage with the Lord. Some of her writing has been published. Some will remain just hers—expressions of her emotions to her best friend, the Lord Jesus. Early on she made Christ her confidant.

Mother has never been tempted by the need for status or acquiring things. She is now surprised to be told that the things she has enjoyed collecting have grown to be valuable—like her primitive antiques she bought, because they were less expensive, to furnish the old log house she had built out of salvage. Old things have always appealed to her and make her feel at home. She has a strong distaste for the new. With love for old things also came an eye for detail. When I returned with her to China, I began to understand the source for her preferences. Obviously, Chinese culture is ancient, and until the cultural revolution, old things and elderly people were revered. Mother absorbed this appreciation, along with her artistic sensitivity.

She is a collector of books and through the years has stumbled across some rare and unusual ones that she personally enjoys. She has never understood why people collect books just to decorate a room. Her books are her friends. They show where she has read by her markings, marginal comments, and notations. Her bedside is crowded with books from the latest bestseller, to something on China, to biography, and always nearby, her beloved Bible. When someone once told her he felt guilty if he started one book before finishing the first, she told him she did not. "After all," she said, "you don't finish all the pickles before you open the olives." Her view is that there are times for different things. One day you may need to read something funny, the next day need a mystery, and yet at night you may want a devotional book for comfort. Her reading reflects her interests and needs.

She is also a collector of quotations. There are few situations where she cannot come up with a choice quote from someone she has read. Her favorites are John Trapp [a sixteenth-century biblical scholar], C. S. Lewis, and George MacDonald. One of her favorites is, "No one is useless; they can always serve as a bad example." When asked if she and my father ever argue, she has often said, "When two people agree on everything one of them is unnecessary." One of her favorite quotes is by C. S. Lewis, speaking of George MacDonald: "He seems to have been a playful man, deeply appreciative of all the really beautiful and delicious things that money can buy, but no less content to do without them." Often she quotes George MacDonald saying of himself, "Let me, if I may, be ever welcomed to my room in winter by a glowing hearth, in summer by a vase of flowers; if I may not, let me think how nice they would have been and bury myself in my work." These quotations that she loves are a window to her own attitude and perspective on life.

BOOK LEARNIN'

Betty Frist

*R*uth once remarked that some might look on it as heresy, but that she had talked with Ph.D's who had bored her to death and to high-school dropouts who fascinated her. Ruth has always been greedy for knowledge and is the direct descendant of a very unusual man who, when he fell from his horse one day, acquired a bruise on his head which kept him from speaking in English. But he continued to speak fluently in Latin and Greek.

Ruth told her daughters (all of them married early), "Keep reading and you'll be educated."

Some time ago, a letter Ruth had written to a friend years ago came to light. She wrote, "I am reveling in good books (the Bible, of course)." Then naming several authors, she continued, "Here's a gem from McDonald—'It's only in Him that the soul has room' and 'Oh, the folly of the mind that will explain God before obeying Him.' And don't you love this from Jeremy Taylor, 'He threatens terrible things if we will not be happy.'" Then she quotes an old Russian proverb, "It's not the ocean that drains but the puddle." Enough quotes.

On the lighter side, Ruth was a little concerned that their older son was taking longer to graduate from college than she felt he should (though he was gathering information which has proved invaluable to him in his present work). After he finally graduated, Ruth informed him that one of his cousins had that very day graduated "with honors." Her son said, grinning, "I graduated with relief."

(from *My Neighbors, the Billy Grahams*)

READING, SPEAKING, AND CORRESPONDENCE
RUTH BELL GRAHAM

*L*et me see! I was counting up the other day the books that I am reading, none of which I have finished. For spiritual stimulation, I adore C. S. Lewis and George McDonald. For refreshment, and just plain old blessings, Amy Carmichael. I have a friend who when things get tough says, "This calls for Amy!" A good cross-section of secular and spiritual. Having all these unfinished books around bothered me until I realized that when I go into the pantry, I don't eat all the peas before I start on the asparagus, and I don't eat all the peaches before I start on the apricots, and not all the Vienna sausage before I start on the tuna fish. In other words, I don't always need the same book the same day. So there is a whole row of them that I can read, depending on the circumstance.

I don't plan to do any more speaking. I just don't feel called to speak. If I had to take a choice between speaking and writing, I would put everything I had to say in a book and let people read it, and I wouldn't have to get up and say it. And in the spring, gardening. That's my therapy, to get out in the flowers and work. I just love it! There are so many things I'd like to do. I love to cook.

There is no typical day. I try to work on letters in the morning. But every day is full of interruptions and I have to play this by ear. I think one thing that a busy housewife and mother has to learn is to accept interruptions as from the Lord. And the sooner she learns it, the happier she'll be. When you do, then you roll with the punches, and each interruption is an opportunity. In other words, if I tried to keep a rigid schedule, every interruption would make me frustrated and irritated. But when I accept each interruption as from the Lord, life becomes much more interesting and much more relaxed.

I try to handle my correspondence half a day each day. Most people write in about problems, and I am not at all sure that they couldn't be handled better by, say, some minister in the person's hometown. All I know is what they write. There may be another side. The only thing I can do is try to point them to the Lord. If they are in a right relationship with Jesus Christ and will take their problem to Him and try to learn all He has to teach them through that problem, that's all they need. It's not that the problem is going to be solved; some problems are unsolvable.

It's not easy to sit down and answer a letter from someone who's facing a tragedy. You just can't send a form letter. Sometimes it takes a whole morning on one letter, with time out to answer the telephone and things like that. So they pile up.

(from an interview with Wesley Pippert)

FOOTPRINTS OF CREATIVITY

When you walk around her house you can see the footprints of her creativity everywhere—her humor and personality.

—KITTY PETERSON

Ruth Could Always Write

She could always write. In high school we had to write a poem, and if it wasn't for her pulling every word out of me I could never have passed.

—GAY CURRIE FOX

Insights

I love her way with words, her insights into things.

—LEIGHTON FORD

Always a Pen and Notebook

Ruth almost always has a pen and an open notebook beside her when she reads the Bible. Just holding the pen is an act of faith, faith that there will be something new to learn or a passage that relates to what she is feeling or thinking about. She records in her notebooks her reactions to the Bible passages she has studied.

Whenever she stops her Bible reading or other work and looks up, the first thing her eyes rest on is a crown of thorns hanging from a nail pounded into the rough log wall. When she was in Jerusalem a few years ago, the Moslem policeman who was acting as her guide cut a branch from a thorny bush beside the dusty road and shaped it into a crown. Ruth believes that Christ's crown of thorns came from the same kind of bush.

—JULIE NIXON EISENHOWER, *Special People*

Writing for Billy

When Billy was a pastor in Illinois he had a radio program, and he asked me to help because he said he wasn't very good at it. But he was quite good at it. He sat at a table in a fifty-thousand-watt station. And from 10:15 to 11:00 on Sunday evening, *Songs in the Night* would be on the air. The program is still on the air with another sponsorship. He found out from me what songs the quartet would be doing, what songs I'd be doing, and Ruth would write two or three lines as introductions. Billy said, "Ruth helps me. She writes a couple of lines to read, and I just take off from there," and he would then talk four or five minutes before the next song. He could do it so beautifully.

—GEORGE BEVERLY SHEA

Ruth's Handwriting

*T*here is only one person I know with that distinctive penmanship, and although we are not related by blood, all my life I have called her Aunt Ruth. She once started a letter by saying, "Can't read my writing? Join the club; neither can I."

—Betty Ruth Barrows Seera

Ruth's handwriting is as unusual as she is. A friend commented, "I'd recognize it if I saw it on a scrap of paper in the Sahara Desert. It's a beautiful script; but if a person isn't familiar with it, he might end up with his eyes crossed after trying to read one of her letters."

One friend tells that her husband called her from his office and said, "There's a letter here for you from Ruth. I'd read it to you over the phone, but I don't have time for a headache."

—Betty Frist, *My Neighbors, the Billy Grahams*

I've teased her a little bit because I think she has the world's hardest to read handwriting. That's her only fault.

—Barbara Bush

Chapter Eleven

WRITING

A poem, a sentence, causes us to see ourselves. I be, and I see my being, at the same time.

—RALPH WALDO EMERSON, *Journals*

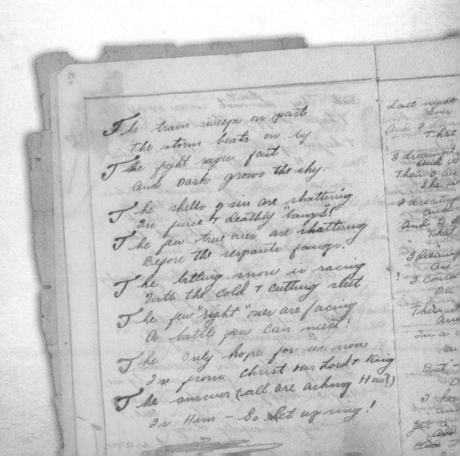

WORKING FOR RUTH
EVELYN FREELAND

*J*n 1966 T. W. Wilson asked me if I would be interested in coming to Montreat to work. So, I started in May of 1966 working for both T. W. and Ruth, which I did all through the years. It worked because Ruth didn't want to do anything in the office while the men were home. And when Mr. Graham was away, Mr. Wilson was away, so it worked for thirty-six years.

It's My Turn revealed a lot more of Ruth as a person to the general public than people had ever known. She'd been seen occasionally with Mr. Graham on television, and there were glimpses of Ruth, but her writings revealed her heart to the public more than anything.

Whenever she was writing she was thinking of others, how she could minister to others or how she could be an encouragement. I presumed and felt from the correspondence following her publications that people saw them as a family like any other family with happy days and challenging days, and that was revealed in her writings. In many ways, she wasn't any different than anyone else, except for the public part of their life. She always had others in mind when she wrote. She wanted it to be a ministry and whenever anybody wanted to use her material, or quote her or whatever, she always gave her permission for that because she wanted it to be a ministry. If something she had written could appear in someone's church bulletin and be a blessing to others, that was her desire. She wrote for ministry, not for money. Their lives have centered on ministering in whatever way they could.

Through the years, on many occasions, she wrote poetry about tough times with the kids, meeting an interesting person, whatever brought something to mind. The writing part goes back to her childhood. She wrote poetry and kept journals her whole life.

Also, in earlier years she did a lot of writing to the children that I typed up with carbon copies—family letters that went to all of them. She described things up on the mountain. I remember one particular observation that some trees lose their leaves from the ground up and others lose theirs from the top down. It's something I had never noticed before. She was very cognizant of things going on around her on the mountain that she loves.

We never worked with a schedule. Ruth didn't keep office hours. We would work when she felt like it. She'd call and ask me to come up the mountain and work. It wasn't a daily thing.

She did a lot of encouraging people. She is a great encourager. She has a positive attitude about everything.

WORKING WITH RUTH

RICHARD JESSE WATSON

I watched Billy Graham on television when I was about fifteen, and at the time I was an atheist and my family were atheists. Mr. Graham had on white shoes and a white belt, and I thought I'd just watch for laughs. But it was so powerful that I got down on my knees and asked Christ into my life. I didn't know what to do with it after that but finally found faith in God.

As an artist I thought I had to do something with my art, so I gave it to God. I said, "I'll do art for You, God." But it seemed like God was saying, "Give it to Me. Just give it up because it seems like it has such an important place in your life." So I gave it up. I was willing never to do it again and just wanted my life to be in the balance.

A couple of years later I was doing a lot of other jobs, working on a farm, milking cows, picking apples, serving as a letter carrier and welder, and you name it. But it seemed God was giving my art back to me, because I wasn't so possessive of the gift. It had died like a seed in the ground and had come back to life.

I realized what I wanted to do was children's books. The first book I did was the illustrations for James Dickey's *Bronwen and the Shape-Shifter* (Harcourt, Brace, and Jovanovich). My dedication in the book says, "To Jesu, the joy of my desiring" because I loved Bach and I wanted to give this first book to God.

That was the book that Steve Griffith brought, with two other books by other illustrators, to show Ruth the kind of things in picture books. He wanted to show her illustrations to get her to see the potential for turning her rendering of the Christmas story into a good picture book. She pointed to mine and said, "That's the artist I want." So Steve called me and it just really blew my mind. You give something to God and He might give it back or He might not. In my case, He gave it back in the form of working with this amazing lady.

She was just a kick to work with. She was so kind. For instance, I was working in this little trailer up in the mountains and woods of California. It was snowing and freezing while I worked on these paintings. I didn't have heating but tried to wrap myself up the best I could. I wrote her a little quote from Winnie the Pooh about how cold my toes were growing or something. I didn't mean to be whining, but she sent me a little heater and it came in pretty handy.

She was so encouraging and so sensitive. When I was having a particular problem, I would call her. She understands the creative process, that it is a process where you struggle and there's angst and there is just no other way to do it. I knew she understood because, obviously, her work shows the beauty that comes out of pain, loneliness, and time alone.

The project with Ruth that I was able to be part of was the *One Wintry Night* book. When we started working together she had only one major request: She wanted the crucifixion scene to be a certain way. She wanted to show the crucifixion from behind. She wanted to show all the nations of the world in the faces of people who stood before the cross. It was a great idea but it would have taken at least a year to paint that one picture. So we finally simplified it.

I tell people she's a visionary. She thinks way ahead (and above) a lot of people.

There was a spot illustration of a cat by this cool lamp with a suit of armor. And I thought that lamp said something about her house. For expediency, I painted my cat. Ruth said, "My cat's not that fancy, Richard. Why don't you just paint my cat, Chester." Well, I had already painted the picture and wanted to say, "I can't do that; it will take me two weeks to do it all over again." But I thought, *Well now, wait a second, if I do what she wants I've got some leverage so if she asks me to do something that's a real pain, I can bargain.* The project was a real collaboration, because it is a marriage of text and art. So I said, "OK, I'll put your cat in," so I scratched the cat off the painting and replaced it with Chester. But I also hid Chester in all the other paintings in the book, except the crucifixion which was just too heavy of a painting. So, if you look close, there is a cat hidden in every painting.

She's so self-effacing. So honest. You can't help but love her. She's like your mother, your grandmother, your best friend. She's such a nut.

For me, her greatest legacy is the way she honors everyone. You feel like you are special when you meet her. You are a gift to the world because she appreciates you for who you are. She cherishes everybody. She's not impressed with status, fame, or position. She's impressed with people who love God and want to serve Him and want to know Him. She helps people to discover who they are. She's been an incredible encouragement to me and to my whole family, and I think that's true of everybody who gets to know her. She builds them up and helps them become that person they want to be and are trying to be and are not sure just how to get there. And she's done this probably millions of times.

When I first met her I said, "Ruth, since this is for children, I can't very well paint Adam and Eve in this super-realism." She replied, "I don't see how anyone can be offended by two little brown bottoms in the distance." So I put two little brown bottoms in the distance and used a lot of plants. So I said, "Well, that's the next question. What do they look like?" She said, "Well, I think the Scripture suggests they're from what is now Iraq." "I don't know," I replied. "I think anthropology suggests it is North Africa." So we went back and forth about this and duked it out. Finally I said, "You know, they probably look a little like every one of us. What I need to do is figure out how to mix together everyone you could think of and blend them together. After I painted those paintings, *Time* magazine came out with an article where they had morphed the different nationalities to show the new face of the nation and a lot of those morphed images looked exactly liked my pictures. I think she was happy with it.

WHAT READERS SAY

It's My Turn

⏤ *It's My Turn* is one of my favorite books! The pages are tattered from use. Ruth Graham applies her faith in real life situations. She is funny, "real," and transparent.

Each chapter is a short story with a truth she has learned and now shares. It is a quick read or a daily devotional. Almost every mother and wife will be able to identify with her wonderful anecdotes.

⏤ *It's My Turn* shares the battles, joys, questions, disappointments, and hope of a woman in the limelight. The struggles of raising children . . . part time alone. I read it on the phone to my elderly mother at night . . . but read so long, it only lasted two nights!

Legacy of a Pack Rat

⏤ Like the proverbial pack rat—filling his lair with bits and pieces of this and that—Ruth Bell Graham has rummaged around in her mental attic and come up with 132 bits and pieces of this and that to share with her readers. Each tiny chapter is filled with vignettes, anecdotes, poems, and quotes that somehow join together to give an intimate portrait of the life and times of this inspiring woman of faith. You could easily use this book like a devotional and just read one tiny section a day, or you could sit down and read the whole thing in one sitting (as I did!). The bits and pieces range the entire gamut: from the deeply profound (like the one about the Chinese executioner who discovered that God could forgive even murder), to the merely amusing (like the one about the time the Grahams served a bowl of "tadpole soup" to a family friend). And, like a day spent digging through the attic looking for secret treasure, it's well worth the effort spent—once you find it.

One Wintry Night

— Ruth Bell Graham does a wonderful job telling the whole story. She has taken you back to the reason for Christmas. Yes, Christmas is the birth of the Christ child, but Ruth has gone to the root of it all! Had there been no Creation, no sin, no Fall, there would not have been a need for the Christ child!

— Everything about this book is lovely—the story and the art-work. You could spend a long time just studying all the pictures. Ruth Bell Graham writes about a grandmotherly woman who offers a warm place for a child to get in out of a snowstorm. She opens her Bible and tells him a fascinating story that begins with Creation and ends with the Resurrection. I purchase this book all the time to give as baptismal gifts. I'd also highly recommend it for anyone sharing their faith with an adult who grew up biblically illiterate. It's a fun, easy way to cover the basics in a way anyone can understand.

— A young boy is lost in the woods one wintry night and is res-cued by a woman who brings him into a warm, cozy cabin. By the blazing fire she quiets him and weaves through his imagination the story of a child who fulfilled the promise God had made from the beginning of the world.

— The story as told to a young boy is wonderful and can cer-tainly stand on its own, but combined with the artwork it is a sure winner. After reading the book, I went back and examined each pic-ture. They are all beautiful. We are adding this to our home library (a Christmas present); I recommend that you do the same.

— I was first drawn to *One Wintry Night* by the illustrations, which are amazing. Realistic pictures give a younger child a lot to look at while you are reading the story. Once I started reading the story, I was in awe. Mrs. Graham retells the story of the Bible in a simple but captivating way. It is easy to see the parallels that occur in the Bible—the way God looked for someone to save His people repeatedly—ending with our Savior. The book intertwines the importance of not only the birth of Christ, but also His crucifixion and resurrection. Mrs. Graham also writes wonderful cliffhangers from one chapter to the next, which had my five-year-old begging to read more. This is definitely a book I will read over and over again and will recommend to my friends (or buy it for them!). This is a great way to help introduce a young child to God's character, the Bible, and Christianity.

— This book shows the Bible to be one story . . . the story of a loving God saving a fallen people. It's a GREAT perspective. The illustrations are beautiful, and the story very well written. I read this to my kids every Christmas, one chapter per night. . . . They're always begging for more! It's wonderful for Christmas, but the story is so much more than just a Christmas story! Highly recommended!

— In a Christmas book you'll never forget, Ruth Bell Graham magnificently blends contemporary settings with the history of God's redeeming love. A story that will fascinate both young and old.

Prodigals and Those Who Love Them
— I have had this book in my library for years, and it is a great source of encouragement. Mrs. Graham's insightful way of sharing her heart with others fans the flame of hope. This is "my" book to give to others whose children are "in the far country."

— I found the book to be a very encouraging word in a time of need when my teenage son had turned his back on the Lord. Ruth's words were helpful and insightful. It was a nice reminder that others have gone through the same or similar thing and come out the other side victorious in the Lord.

⌐ Ruth Bell Graham writes about famous historical men who lived rebellious lives before submitting to the Lordship of Jesus Christ. She gives parents hope as she unravels these men's crooked paths and shows how in the end they were used mightily of God. In between these chapters she interjects her own words, poems, and prayers of encouragement taken from her many years of journaling during her own son's rebellious times. She unveils the pain of a mother's heart and at the same time gives great hope for all readers to trust God to do amazing things with their own children. Ruth Bell Graham stresses the need to turn our "borrowed" children over to God and let Him do His work—and often that work is in our own lives first.

Collected Poems

⌐ I first discovered Ruth Bell Graham's poetry in her book titled *Sitting by My Laughing Fire,* now out of print, in the early 80s. I have searched for that edition in resale shops and garage sales to share her gift of expression with friends. I have enclosed copies of individual poems from it in notes to friends at times of celebration and sadness because Mrs. Graham is able to concisely convey feelings of joy and empathy. *Collected Poems* contains many of the verses from the earlier collection and others as well which spring from her rich life.

Footprints of a Pilgrim

⌐ Like Graham herself, there's plenty of humor here, and just a spark of mischief, whether it's her memories of breaking curfew in college and getting grounded ("I found I had plenty of time to write"), or her thoughts on marriage ("Divorce never . . . murder maybe").

Peppered throughout are short, boxed vignettes about Ruth written by her children, her husband, one-time neighbor and crime novelist Patricia Cornwell, author Jan Karon, and former First Lady Barbara Bush. By turns poignant, humorous, and wistful, this scrapbook memoir is a fitting salute to an admired personality.

— I have not finished the book, but already I know I must have it to read over and over the rest of my life. I am sorry for the person who doesn't enjoy her poetry. Ruth Graham's poetry is the first I've enjoyed, and she offers so much of herself in it. I urge everyone to sit by a laughing fire and read this book, along with Ruth's other delightful works.

— I am currently memorizing the Readers Theatre version of *Footprints of a Pilgrim.* The book has made me laugh, cry, and think back over my life. The perseverance and strength of Ruth Bell Graham have been an inspiration to me. The theatre group I work with will be performing this drama. It is an honor to be able to portray the life of such a wonderful Christian woman. I'm sure this book will bless any reader.

It's a beautiful book, combining pictures from throughout her life with biography and poetry. I'm not a big fan of her poetry, so I tended to skim those sections. But the biographical portion offers a comprehensive look at her life from childhood in China to student days at Wheaton College to wife and mother. Her faith and wit shine through in vignettes contributed by her children and friends. We have a lot to learn from Mrs. Graham's generation, and this book will help to preserve her wisdom long after she's gone.

MISCELLANEOUS QUOTES ON BOOKS

Never Interested in Reviews

She was never much interested in reviews of her books. She didn't toot her own horn; she didn't care. With *It's My Turn* she agreed to do one publicity trip, and I went with her on that. It was a special time, a fun weekend. We went to New York and she appeared on the *Today Show* for about two minutes, then we flew to L.A. and she was on the *Merv Griffin* show. That's all. Sales of the books have never concerned her.

—EVELYN FREELAND

One Wintry Night

My kids love *One Wintry Night*. We read it every year. They look and look for the hidden cat.

—BERDJETTE TCHIVIDJIAN BARKER

Prodigals and Those Who Love Them

Prodigals is the book that brought the most mail from the public. They loved the encouragement of the book and knowing that the Grahams had gone through similar situations in their home. It struck a chord. She always got lots of mail when the books were published, but that one brought the most.

—EVELYN FREELAND

Chapter Twelve

POETRY

I've written because, at the time, I had to. It was write or develop an ulcer. I chose to write.

—RUTH BELL GRAHAM, INTRODUCTION TO *Collected Poems*

RUTH BELL GRAHAM'S POETRY

JAN KARON

Ruth Graham's work possesses what I believe to be the hallmark of great poetry: It is intensely personal, yet also distinctly universal.

I urge you to demonstrate the truth of this observation by reading her poetry alone, hugging it to yourself. Then, read it aloud to your family, as Charles Dickens's devoted readers eagerly read his work aloud to their families. The depth and nuance of her passion will not only thrill and move you privately, it will come alive in the imaginations of your loved ones in ways that have the power to touch.

Since reading poetry at all, much less aloud, is hardly our national pastime, you may wonder: Is Ruth Graham's poetry like the stuff you read in school—too hard, too obscure, too odd to grapple with? Never! In her work, you'll hear a voice you may sometimes recognize as your own—that of a wife, a mother, a sweetheart, a child, a woman, an adventurer, a visionary, and even, occasionally, a doubter. Ruth Graham has many voices, and she doesn't try to hide or disguise even one of them.

Would we dare to be so open, so transparent, if we were the wife of a man who's known and loved the world over? Ruth Graham has dared. She has dared, however, not because she wanted to or thought she should, but because she couldn't help it.

These poems are dear to my heart. I've read them alone—and to others—for a long time now. It is always a joy to sit by this poet's laughing fire or to walk with her through the crisp, loud leaves of fall, watching mist curl among the hills of Little Piney Cove.

What Ruth Graham's poetry does for me and has for a very long time (and I hope Ruth understands what I mean by this), is make it feel as if it were my own, as if in fact in some strange way I had written it myself.

I can't say I read her poetry well, but in my inner ear I hear it as coming forth very naturally, again, as if it were my own. I think that anyone who enjoys reading at all (and perhaps they haven't been able to read other poetry because it is too dense, too thick, too veiled) will enjoy her poetry. There is no veil over Ruth Graham's poetry. This woman has had the courage to lay herself bare on the page.

Ruth Graham, married to one of the most famous men who ever lived, is unafraid to let you know that she has suffered. She's unafraid to let you know she feels depression and pain and anguish. I love that in her.

I love her complete openness, her lack of any timidity about showing you who she is. And it's not always a pretty picture. She pleads with God in a number of her poems. It's like, "Stop already." "Please, let this be over." "Give me a break here, God." This is the way the old Jews spoke to God. They conversed with God. His name is Emmanuel, God with us, and so often in her poetry I sense that God is right there. She is talking to Him. This is a two-way street.

So Ruth Graham's poetry is vital to me. It's full of flesh and blood.

Another thing I love about her poetry is that it is so visual. She can take me out-of-doors just like that.

It must be hard for her to write but it feels like it just flows out of her without effort. I can see the effort in some poetry and I don't like to see the effort.

I've had the privilege and delight of meeting Ruth Graham in person, of sitting with her and Dr. Graham in their living room while they held hands like teenage sweethearts. It is her poetry, however, that enables me to say that I've not only met Ruth Graham, but know her.

IN HER POETRY YOU SEE HER SOUL

*S*o many of my friends have asked me if they could spend time with Mother just to sit around in the living room, have tea, and talk. But I realized they can't. The only way I could really share her with other women is to encourage her writing or to share what she has taught me through my writing. Mother is such a balanced, fun-loving Christian with a wonderful sense of humor. She has a wonderful way of looking at life. She's a great example to other women of how to be an authentic Christian woman.

If you read Mother's prose you get the funny stories, you get her sense of humor, but in her poetry you see her soul.

—GIGI GRAHAM TCHIVIDJIAN

A Tremendous Legacy

She's left a tremendous legacy in her beautiful prose and poetry for us to enjoy. I find a lot of peace and wisdom in what she has to say about this world and how to live in it.

—KARLENE SHEA

Expressing Her Feelings

Ruth is an extremely private person. They've kept personal things in. Billy told me that once he shared something really deep and personal with a minister friend, and it was a very confidential thing. He said within two weeks the whole country knew about it.

They do not express feelings very much. Ruth gets her feelings out through her poetry and her writing.

—JEAN GRAHAM FORD

Her Poems Are My Friends

When they first dramatized her poetry in the stage presentation *Footprints of a Pilgrim,* I suddenly realized something. I knew I loved her poetry—I'd given it to lots of people—but suddenly I realized these poems were my friends. They were my friends, my buddies, and I identified with so many. So many people do.

—KARLENE SHEA

SITTING BY MY LAUGHING FIRE

*S*itting by My Laughing Fire." I was so in tune with that phrase from one of her poems. We shared a lot of things together. I understood "Sitting by My Laughing Fire" so well, because it is the best company in the world.

—CLAUDIA (LADY BIRD) JOHNSON

Sitting by my laughing fire
I watch the whitening world without,
and hear the wind climb higher, higher,
rising to a savage shout;
and on my hearth
the logs smile on,
warming me
as they slowly perish;
they had been felled
by ax and saw
while fellow trees
were left to flourish;
but what was spared
by ax and saw,
by some unspoken,
cruel law,
was being harvested without
by ice and wind and savage shout.
And on my hearth
the logs smile on.

—RUTH BELL GRAHAM

Ruth's Sensitivity

"I'm Daniel Creasman's Mother" shows how sensitive Ruth is to people of all descriptions. She likes characters and she sees characters everywhere.

—Calvin Thielmann

"I'm Daniel Creasman's mother. I brung these clothes
so's you
could dress him up real natural-like—
no . . .
navy wouldn't do.
He liked this little playsuit—
it's sorta faded now—
that tore place he
he got tryin'
to help his daddy plow.
No . . .
if he dressed real smart-like—
and all that fancy trim—
the last we'd see of Danny,
it wouldn't seem
like him.
But . . .
comb his hair. . . real special . . .
(if 'twouldn't seem
too odd) . . .
I brush it so
come Sunday
when he goes
to the house of God."
That afternoon
I saw him—

so still, so tanned he lay—
with the faded blue suit on him,
like he'd just come in from play. . .
but his hair was brushed
"real special" . . .
and it didn't seem
one bit odd, for . . .
he was just a small boy,
done with play
gone home to the house of God.

—RUTH BELL GRAHAM

Typing for a Perfectionist

*L*ong before computers I typed her poetry and manu-
scripts. She would redo minute little details, a change
of word, or punctuation. She was tenacious about wanting things
exactly the way she wanted them. Her favorite punctuation was
comma dash. Publishers didn't like that. But she stuck with it.
Recently, I saw a comma dash on something I read and thought,
Ruth's not the only one who did that. She would refine things over and
over, obviously still thinking about the piece. She was a stickler for
detail she wanted.

I love the things she wrote about seeing things around the house.
In the fall I always think about her "candle flames" of poplars. I
watch the trees and think about Ruth.

—Evelyn Freeland

Give me a cove—
a little cove—
when Fall comes
amblin' round:
hint of frost
upon the air,
sunlight
on the ground;
a little cove
with poplars—
calm
and
straight

and
tall;
to burn like candle flames
against
the sullen gray
of Fall.
P. S.
We bought this cove
when coves were cheap,
flatland scarce,
mountains steep.
Not once
were we ever told
in autumn
poplars
turn to gold.

—RUTH BELL GRAHAM

My Grandmother's Poetry

There's so many levels to the poem I like the best ("And When I Die"). I'm sure it speaks to different people different ways. But what I love about the poem is that normally we're told that our lives on earth are just earthly stuff, but it's your heavenly life that counts. But in the poem she says on the other hand, it does count on earth. I love the picture of her rising slowly and just looking at her life with a different perspective. It gives me the sense that she enjoys life but knows there's more to come.

For me the poem came to life from the Reader's Theatre production, *Footprints of a Pilgrim*. The poem brought the whole show about her life into perspective.

—BERDJETTE TCHIVIDJIAN BARKER

And when I die
I hope my soul ascends
slowly, so that I
may watch the earth receding
out of sight,
its vastness growing smaller
as I rise,
savoring its recession
with delight.
Anticipating joy
is itself a joy.
And joy unspeakable
and full of glory
needs more
than "in the twinkling of an eye,"
more than "in a moment."
Lord, who am I to disagree?
It's only we
have much to leave behind;
so much . . . Before.
These moments
of transition
will, for me, be
time
to adore.

—RUTH BELL GRAHAM

Chapter Thirteen

PERSEVERANCE AND PAIN

Language has created the word *loneliness* to express the pain of being alone, and the word *solitude* to express the glory of being alone.

—PAUL TILLICH

LIFE HAS NOT BEEN EASY

RUTH GRAHAM MCINTYRE

*L*ife has not been easy for Mother. With five children to raise, a home to run, a husband rarely home and usually far away, and the world watching for any flaws and expecting her to be perfect, she has experienced her share of sorrows, burdens, injustice, confusion, pressure, and hurt. However, I would not say that I have ever seen Mother display anger or doubt. As a single mother, I am now viewing my mother with new eyes. With the heavy responsibility of family, a home to run, bills to pay, not enough money to meet the demands, being expected to act and dress appropriately although she was never trained for her position, a husband who was married to his ministry and often preoccupied, she maintained her perspective. How did she do it? Early on she made Christ her center.

One of the deep sorrows of my mother's life occurred when she had to leave the shelter of her home, that secure compound, and go away to northern Korea to high school. She has often said that God was then preparing her for a lifetime of good-byes. But to a young thirteen-year-old girl whose heart was breaking with homesickness, she had no idea what God's purposes would be and therefore turned to the One she knew she could trust above all others, her heavenly Father. Early in her life she made Christ her home.

What she witnessed in her family home, she now practiced for herself—dependence on God in every circumstance, love for His Word, concern for others above self, and an indomitable spirit displayed with a smile. Self-sacrifice was a way of life. Horatio K. F. Eden once described another in a way that aptly describes Mother: "I never knew her to fail to find happiness wherever she was placed and good in whomever she came across. Whatever the circumstances might be, they always yielded to her causes for thankfulness and work to be done with a ready and hopeful heart."

When I left home at age thirteen and was torn by homesickness, her well-worn advice was for me to look around to find someone who was more homesick than I was and cheer her up. Mother's weekly letters to me were full of news and always encouraging. She never failed to close a letter by telling me she loved me and was praying for me.

THE INFAMOUS ZIP LINE
BERDJETTE TCHIVIDJIAN BARKER

I was pretty young, perhaps third grade, but I have vivid memories of standing underneath this very large tree. I'm sure someone had gotten it in my grandmother's head that we needed a zip line because we had one in Europe when we lived there. (I don't know if she was behind that one or not.) My grandmother was instrumental in getting all the parts and all of us putting it together. When it was all up, all of us kids were standing under the tree and the thought of climbing up that high scared us. It was too high for us. So we said, "Teh-Teh, Teh-Teh, you do it, you do it first." So the good sport she is, she climbed up there to do it. As soon as she hung on, immediately it just fell to the ground. I remember her lying there and just kind of moaning and all of us laughing. "Oh come on, Teh-Teh." She was such a jokester we thought she was just playing around and joking and making these noises and such. I don't remember much after that. I don't even remember knowing how serious it was and that she was in a coma. I do remember her going to the hospital and doctors being involved and that's all. I always feel a little bad that we made her do it.

I have a very vivid picture of that tree and the zip line.

SPIRITUAL STAMINA

*W*e speak of her humor and her delightful way of saying things, but we do remember also 1975 being unreal. Billy received a call that Ruth had visited the grandchildren in Milwaukee and had an unfortunate accident while trying to fix a swing. She fell on the hard ground. And there was a very kind physician who kept informing Billy several times a day how she was doing. From that accident in 1975 she developed pain which would reoccur. But through it all, we all remember that smile and when one would ask, "How are you doing, Ruth?" "Just fine." That's spiritual stamina.

—GEORGE BEVERLY SHEA

Loss of Consciousness

Her ability to draw on passages from the Bible has often helped her in moments of crisis. Years ago when she fell out of a tree while trying to put up a swing and suffered a concussion, she was in pain and terribly confused about dates and events when she eventually regained consciousness. But her greatest distress was her inability to remember the Bible verses she had spent a lifetime learning. For a week, she prayed, *Lord, I can give up anything—but not my Bible verses.* It was more than two weeks after her concussion that somewhere from deep within her mind came the words, "Yea, I have loved thee with an everlasting love: therefore with lovingkindness have I drawn thee." She could not remember what part of the Bible this verse came from and, to this day, she cannot remember when or why she learned this verse from Jeremiah. But as she lay in bed, cherishing these words that had come to her, she knew a sense of great comfort. And she prayed. *Thank You, Lord.*

As the wife of an evangelist, Ruth Bell Graham is expected to be ready and willing to offer spiritual advice to those who write to her and to those who seek her out in person. But there are times when Ruth herself is spiritually bereft: She still believes in God, but finds that she can no longer pray easily and spontaneously. These episodes of what she calls "spiritual dryness" always follow very busy periods when she does not have time to study the Bible on a regular basis. "It is just as if Bill and I get so busy and go for several days and don't sit down and have a good talk," she explained. At that moment I realized how much Ruth has sacrificed to the demands of her husband's ministry. There were many years when she could not travel with her husband because of the children, times when weeks and sometimes months would go by without her having the opportunity for "a good talk" with Billy.

—JULIE NIXON EISENHOWER, *Special People*

Ruth Never Complains

Ruth never complains about pain. If she let you know she was hurting, she was really hurting and that was rare.

The beginning of the various problems through the years was when she fell out of the tree. That was such a severe blow to her body; it couldn't have helped having an impact on her health in the later years.

—EVELYN FREELAND

No Organ Recital

It never ceases to amaze me how she is so able to put up with painful things in her life, whether it is emotional or physical, at such a low point. She's just so willing and eager to help others and love others. I just don't know how in the world she does it.

In twenty-six years, if I ever exasperated Ruth, she never showed it; she never made a sigh or remark. To have the hip pain, the coma from falling out of the tree, the back surgery. She says when you get in certain circles an organ recital starts and everyone starts sharing their aches and pains. But Ruth has never wanted to participate in that. She has never wanted to talk about it and give her own organ recital. It's like she's saying, just because I'm in pain, it's not going to help me by telling someone else I'm hurting.

—MAURIE SCOBIE

I Don't Know How She Does It

Even when she answers the phone, it is always uplifting. I just don't know how she does it. She has tremendous faith and tremendous courage. She's in pain all the time, but you would never know it.

—GAY CURRIE FOX

END OF CONSTRUCTION

*E*nd of Construction: Thank You for Your Patience.
—RUTH BELL GRAHAM'S PROPOSED EPITAPH

Chapter Fourteen

FULL CIRCLE

The wheel has come full circle.
—WILLIAM SHAKESPEARE, *King Lear*

A WARM HUG

BETTY RUTH BARROWS SEERA

*O*h, the pleasure of a personal letter found amidst the bills and appeals that flood my mailbox on a daily basis! Often I know who the letter is from at first glance by the familiar handwriting. This is especially true when I see a bold, black script sloping toward the western edge of the envelope. There is only one person I know with that distinctive penmanship, and although we are not related by blood, all my life I have called her Aunt Ruth. Half print, half cursive, often short, always encouraging, they never fail to deliver their greeting with the "warm hug" with which Aunt Ruth always signs her letters to me. And as I think back on my relationship with her I realize Aunt Ruth has been delivering "warm hugs" to me all of my life.

One of my earliest memories is from a visit I made to Aunt Ruth's home on Little Piney Ridge. The home is actually one very large cabin with room after room of interesting objects, pictures, and books. As a young girl I thought it was a wonderful place. I don't remember now just why I went but I do remember Daddy and Uncle Billy were gone on a long trip and Mama was sick. I also remember that although none of the girls were home at the time, Franklin was, and he teased me mercilessly for the entire visit. Aunt Ruth let me pick the room I wanted to sleep in, and when I awakened in the mornings and looked out upon range after range of the Blue Ridge Mountains, I felt like a princess. The windows had no screens, and I loved leaning out as far as I could to take in the magnificent view. During that visit we went for several hikes on Little Piney Ridge accompanied by her huge dogs. Aunt Ruth knew of several berry patches in these woods where we feasted to our heart's content. I was amazed that she took so much time to be with me.

Her life on that mountain seemed so quiet and peaceful. She talked a lot about her love of books and how she didn't feel lonely when Uncle Billy was gone because she always had a good story for company. I was not much of a reader as a child so this really made an impression on me. I began to suspect it was this passion for reading that made Aunt Ruth so interesting. She seemed to think it was a good use of time, sitting by her fire enjoying her books. Although both of my parents were readers, I didn't often see them take time to sit and read for pleasure. Mama had read great stories to us, but I assumed that growing up meant leaving behind the storybooks to concentrate on more grown-up endeavors. Actually, it makes me laugh to realize just how far I have come in my thinking on this subject. I now consider myself somewhat lost if I do not have my latest book nearby, and I am always excited when I meet someone who reads for the sheer pleasure of a good story. They are a special breed and often a kindred spirit! I am quite sure this love was nurtured by Aunt Ruth's laughing fire.

As I grew up I had fewer opportunities to visit Little Piney Ridge, but when I did, Aunt Ruth never let the visit end without a chat about what we had been reading. More than once she has pulled a book from one of dozens of shelves to send home with me. She has introduced me to some of my favorite authors, and how much I have learned about loving and living from them. These books have become my dear companions, enveloping my mind and heart with the "warm hug" first given by Aunt Ruth so many years ago.

But the sweetest hug of all came later in my life as I watched Aunt Ruth reach out with love and encouragement to my mama as she walked through the valley of the shadow.

Having met as young brides, Mama and Aunt Ruth traveled together with Daddy and Uncle Billy through postwar Europe in the late 40s and early 50s. In those early days of ministry, they shared the excitement and demands that came with their husbands' vision to take the good news of the gospel of Christ around the world. And they shared the vision! As children came along, they unquestioningly accepted the role of single parent for weeks and sometimes months at a time. Of course their homes became very special to these strong-spirited women. They each poured great energy and love into making a warm, comfortable refuge where the five children each had been blessed with could grow in body and spirit, and their travel-weary husbands could rest and refuel.

It was to Mama's home that Uncle Billy and Aunt Ruth came, along with George Beverly and Karlene Shea, when at the age of sixty-five she was diagnosed with advanced breast cancer. I was there at the time, having come to stay with Mama until Daddy could return from his travels. She was released from the hospital in time for his return, and both of them were so excited to have the Grahams and Sheas come to visit. They arrived together, these dear friends, who with Daddy had traveled the world for almost half a century telling the story of Jesus. They greeted each other warmly and enjoyed lunch followed by a long visit by the fire. Very little was said about the upcoming battle with cancer. Instead, they caught up on news about the children and grandchildren and reminisced about the early days of their ministry together. One story led to another, often accompanied by laughter as well as tears as they recounted God's many blessings upon their lives. A big part of that afternoon was spent with Uncle Bev at the piano playing gospel tunes, hymns, and choruses. Sometimes we sang along with him, sometimes we just listened to his deep, comforting voice.

Into the fabric of that day was woven many Scriptures; passages memorized and recited to encourage each other. They would quote whole psalms together, some knowing the hard parts better than others, carrying the group through to the end. Of all the songs, stories, and Scriptures shared that day, it is Aunt Ruth's that I remember most vividly. It came late in the afternoon, after several hours of visiting had passed. With gentle deliberation she broke into a reflective silence with these words: "What shall we then say to these things? If God be for us, who can be against us? He that spared not his own Son, but delivered him up for us all, how shall he not with him also freely give us all things?" [Romans 8:31–32]. She went on to recite the rest of Romans 8: "Who shall separate us from the love of Christ? shall tribulation, or distress, or persecution, or famine, or nakedness, or peril, or sword? . . . Nay, in all these things we are more than conquerors through him that loved us." When she came to the glorious last verses of that chapter, her voice was strong and confident. "For I am persuaded, that neither death, nor life, nor angels, nor principalities, nor powers, nor things present, nor things to come, nor height, nor depth, nor any other creature, shall be able to separate us from the love of God, which is in Christ Jesus our Lord." These words were almost stunning to me. I had heard them all my life; it was a very familiar passage. I even remembered they were from Romans 8, but never before had I realized the depth of comfort and hope they offered. I determined that day to memorize this passage and to follow Aunt Ruth's example to be ready to give an account for the hope that is within me.

Aunt Ruth visited Mama many more times before the Lord took her home. When Mama's mind was too clouded with pain to comprehend conversation, Aunt Ruth would look through photo albums with her and talk about her family. She wrote wonderful letters of encouragement between these visits, even teased Mama that if she didn't hurry up and go to heaven, Aunt Ruth might just beat her there. "And life will just continue," she wrote. "It will actually just be beginning. We will be all new and eternally young again. We will be able to work forever and never get tired." These letters not only encouraged Mama at the time, they also became windows into

Aunt Ruth's own mind and heart. Her thoughts on heaven and what awaited us there were so clear and full of hope. There is little doubt in my mind that she felt almost envious because Mama was going to get there first. "I think myself that dying can be a drag," she said, "a painful, exhausting, depressing thing. But it is the glory that lies ahead . . ." and there she stopped, leaving to the imagination what is beyond our thinking—eternity with Jesus.

In the years since Mama's death, Aunt Ruth has had a few glimpses of heaven herself. Her health has not been equal to her spirit. The last time I visited Little Piney Ridge she greeted me with a lively smile and warm hug. Though her body reflected the suffering she has endured, her eyes were full of life, her spirit strong and focused. She had fixed a tray for tea and we sat by her warm fire talking of family, books, and how much we miss Mama! This is the sweet gift she still gives me—her love and memories of Mama. And yes, when I left, there was a new book under my arm with that precious inscription inside: "A warm hug, Aunt Ruth."

MOTHERS TOGETHER
GIGI GRAHAM TCHIVIDJIAN

Opening the heavy wooden shutters covering the windows in our small chalet, I gazed in wonder at the beauty before me. It was one of those indescribable spring days that can only be experienced in the Alps. I took in a deep breath of the cool, crisp air rushing in through the open window. The early morning sun was just beginning to reflect off the snow-covered peaks surrounding our valley. The wildflowers strewn over the fields below were ready to burst into a knot of color . . . purple, yellow, blue, mauve.

I turned to look at my small son asleep in his crib and felt the delicate movements of the unborn child within me. I was filled with warm emotion.

Slipping on my robe, I gently gathered my sleeping son in my arms. I found my mother, who had come to share this day with us, in the kitchen. She had already made the café au lait and was slicing the thick, Swiss bread. As we sat together, sipping the hot coffee and eating bread smothered with rich butter and strawberry jam, I was overwhelmed with joy.

Mother reached into her pocket and handed me an envelope. I opened it and discovered her Mother's Day gift to me.

It seems but yesterday
you lay
new in my arms.
Into our lives you brought
sunshine
and laughter—

play—
showers, too,
and song.
Headstrong,
heartstrong,
gay,
tender beyond believing,
simple in faith,
clear-eyed,
shy, eager for life—
you left us
rich in memories,
little wife.
And now today
I hear you say
words wise beyond your years;
I watch you play
with your small son,
tenderest of mothers.
Years slip away—
today
we are mothers
together.

—RUTH BELL GRAHAM

Now Mother and I are not only mothers together but grand-mothers together. Children so quickly grow into parents, parents into grandparents, and grandparents into great-grandparents.

The role of parenting, I thought to myself, is like the ever-widening ripple a stone makes in the quiet waters of a mountain lake. Once you love, you are never free again.

I reflected on all the years of mothering, and I agreed with what

John Trapp said many years ago: "Children are certain cares, uncertain joys."

I smiled to myself. Although the joys have far outweighed the cares and parenthood continues to be my most rewarding occupation, I do not find it easy. Parenting is a huge responsibility; it is demanding physically, emotionally, and spiritually.

My mother was once asked how she had raised five children with my Daddy being away so much of the time.

"On my knees," she replied.

Certainly I have not discovered a better or more effective way to raise children.

We are all parents together, striving to be faithful with responsibilities which God has entrusted to each of us. There are many times we feel overwhelmed or become discouraged. But remember, God is a Father with a mother's heart. When you feel depleted, simply turn to Him and exchange your insufficiency for His all-sufficiency.

With David we can say, "The Lord is my strength . . . my heart trusts in him, and I am helped" (Psalm 28:7 NIV).

Mother is now a great-grandmother many times over, and I am a grandmother of ten and counting. Time passes quickly! Much more quickly than we ever expected. Recently, I was at home in Florida when the phone rang.

"Hello?" I answered.

"Gigi, honey, this is Daddy."

"Hi, Daddy, how are you?" I asked cheerfully.

"Well, I am not too good, honey. Mother is real sick and I was wondering if you could come home."

"What's wrong?" I asked anxiously, sensing real concern in his voice.

"Mother is so bad that we have had to take her to the hospital.

She is running a very high temperature and they don't know what is wrong. Could you possibly come home on the next plane?" he asked.

I could tell that he was quite distressed and worried.

"Well, of course, Daddy. I will be there as quickly as I can make arrangements," I responded. I was on a plane and at home in North Carolina by that evening. Mother was extremely ill, and I stayed with her for many weeks. It was very emotional to see her in intensive care for so long. But it was just as emotional, if not more so, to see Daddy so worried and so lost without her.

Through this experience and others, I have begun to understand coming "full circle."

Helping to care for my parents is a responsibility and a privilege that I would not trade for anything.

Yes, at times it is difficult, and it is not always convenient. Often I have to make tough choices between the needs of my husband, the children, the grandchildren, or my elderly parents, especially my mother. But oh, the privilege and the joy of giving back a small portion to Mother of what she has given to me.

(from *Mothers Together*)

THE MOST UNFORGETTABLE CHARACTER I'VE EVER KNOWN

STEPHEN GRIFFITH

APRIL 17, 2003

*A*s my wife and I started up to the Grahams' house, I was reminded of Betty Frist's description of the "scalloped, tortuous mountain road, sometimes called 'Coronary Hill' [where] your car will strain up and around like a broken arrow." I know the first few times I ventured up to the house on my own I got lost. Now I can drive up focusing on the scenery instead of the twists and turns. Spring bloomed with gorgeous deep pink-shaded tulips decorating the well-kept lawns.

We passed the hand-lettered "Watch Out for Falling Rocks" sign, then two large boulders that slipped onto the driveway years ago. There were two reasons I was thankful that I could again see these sights: (1) Ruth was feeling better, and (2) she wanted to work on a book.

As I pulled up to the house, the guard dogs ran up to the car. Over the years I've seen quite a few of these dogs come and go. I told my wife, "Highly trained guard dogs come up here, but Mrs. Graham turns them into sweet, friendly pets in no time."

We opened the front door and yelled, "Hello? Anybody home?" We were greeted by Theresa, assisting Mrs. Graham that day.

As we walked through the familiar hall, past the *One Wintry Night* painting of Moses and Pharaoh, and into the living room, Mrs. Graham was seated on the couch, stunning in a stylish peach jacket with a long black skirt. Both Lorraine and I leaned over to give her a big kiss and hug, careful to be gentle with her frail body.

After sitting down nearby, I noticed the fire in the fireplace was not lit but had been prepared. In earlier days she would have jumped up and lit the fire, but I knew because of her hip problems she was no longer able to get up and move around by herself.

Although she was eager to get down to business, she paused and made a point of asking about our lives, our dogs, and our projects.

The impetus for the meeting was her desire to revise *Prodigals and Those Who Love Them.* Ruth wanted to simplify *Prodigals,* taking out most of the content, paring it down to a few simple ideas. We batted around the possibilities. I challenged a few of her proposals and she defended them. It was a familiar scene and one of the joys of my life—the process of hammering out the book, making sure our plan is solid. After that, it's up to me to try to get the ideas implemented and in print. This time was no different. I agreed to do my best.

We then talked about the possibility of a couple of new projects, as well as the publisher's proposal to make a smaller book out of *One Wintry Night.* After disposing of these topics, I courageously brought up the book you're reading (which she had forgotten about) and began to explain my concept of unveiling her life chronologically— through many sets of eyes, hoping people could create a unique picture of her life and work.

She seemed a little cautious about the whole thing, but I pushed forward. I told her I was thankful she didn't like reading about herself, because she probably wouldn't take the time to make corrections in the book. She laughed, and I started reading.

I skipped over my introduction and started with the stories. She would nod, smile, and we would often stop and laugh together. Following are a few of the observations Ruth made about some of the anecdotes included:

- She confirmed that Maurie Scobie organized the attic when he first came to Montreat, but added, "I haven't been able to find some things since."

- After hearing Berdjette's description of the mysterious attic, Ruth said she also hung two black snakeskins over the doorway to keep everyone out.
- She laughed out loud at the story of Franklin and the matches, and with a twinkle in her eye said, "That's him!"
- When she heard Berdjette's story about the zip line, she didn't take time to confirm the details of the story but instead began to explain how we could build one at our house. She began detailing the need of a strong cable with a handlebar type contraption on the end—starting high but being able to walk by the end of the ride. It seemed like she would enjoy directing the construction of another one.
- Ruth was touched by the comments from former First Ladies Barbara Bush and Lady Bird Johnson, and mentioned she spoke with Linda Johnson Robb and Lady Bird the previous day and was determined to call Barbara Bush to tell her what she thought of her son's leadership over the past few weeks of the war in Iraq.
- Mrs. Graham listened intently to Betty Ruth Barrows Seera's contribution and smiled as she remembered the sweet times of sharing with Betty Ruth's mom, wincing at the mention of her friend's pain. By the end of the piece, we were all fighting back tears.

We continued talking long after I finished reading. I told her I had two lingering questions. The first one was, since she was one of the belles of Wheaton, how did Billy ever have the courage to ask her out? She answered, "He exaggerated that part about me being a belle of Wheaton" and she had been "attracted to him when she heard him pray once in the library at college, before they met." That's what drew her to him.

I also asked, "Some say they never heard you and Mr. Graham argue. How could that be when I know you love a good argument?"

She laughed and said, "We did have disagreements, but I had a closed-door policy, and we took our disagreements out of hearing." This led to our talking about her kids, and I mentioned I had a renewed appreciation for all of her children after listening to their interviews.

Ruth then talked about her thankfulness to God for each of her children (Gigi, Anne, Franklin, Ruth, and Ned) and how they loved God with all of their hearts, in spite of her and Billy's shortcomings as parents.

As she continued talking, I pushed away the thought that there probably wouldn't be too many more times this scene would be repeated. I know the Grahams accept death and believe God will call them "home" when He wants them . . . and not a minute earlier. But I'm afraid I will not handle their deaths well.

Instead, I decided to focus on today and Ruth's desire to begin a new project. After all, she recently told Ken Garfield, religion editor at *The Charlotte Observer,* "If I didn't have a project, I think I'd die of boredom. I can't imagine anything more boring than sitting in discomfort and pain and doing nothing."

I thought of her proposed epitaph, "End of Construction: Thank You for Your Patience." Despite her pain, despite her age, she has no intention of giving up. She knows, although her body is in decline, she's still growing, becoming the person God wants her to be. The construction is not complete, and God is not finished with her until He takes her home. It's this attitude about life that is one of the key lessons I've learned from Ruth at these mountaintop experiences.

Before we left, I showed her the picture at the beginning of this book and read the introduction, "Two Photos." She took the photo and broke into a huge smile. With her eyes wide and sparkling she said, "I remember this picture," and went on to describe when it was taken.

While she was talking, I studied her, hardly noticing the more than sixty years difference between the photo and the woman sitting before me. There was that same confidence and humor. The only difference was, knowing more about her life enabled me to see a depth of character a simple photo could never fully reveal.

Finally, I could see she was tiring and Lorraine and I decided to leave. We told Ruth good-bye but that we'd see her in a couple of weeks to begin work on a new book. Then we walked out of the house to the car.

I was silent as we got into the car and started down the mountain. After hearing so many stories about Ruth from others over the months, my mind raced through my own stories. I remembered the day thirteen years ago when visiting with Ruth I got a call from my mother telling me my father had died. The next week at the funeral in the small town in Tennessee where I grew up, a big cross made of white roses was delivered with a simple card from Ruth and Billy Graham. I could not believe this gesture of love and comfort from the Grahams. My mother was also greatly touched by their kindness and spent several months laboring over a needlework proclaiming the names of God she sent to Ruth as a thank you.

Six years later my mother died of cancer. The next time I was visiting Ruth, she left the room and came back with the needlework my mother made and placed it in my hands.

I realized while driving down the mountain that I was not prepared for Ruth's death. I know I will be devastated by her death, despite her own solace in the prospect.

I can only hope that I can continue to grow into such wisdom and care for others. Seeing the way she lives, her love of life, her faith, and her confidence in the future has made an indelible mark on my life that I will carry with me the remainder of my days.

Acknowledgments

Thanks, Ruth, for letting me be a part of your life. Thanks to all those who wrote pieces and were interviewed for this book, and especially to Gigi Graham Tchividjian for being my publishing partner for so many years.

Also thanks to:

My daughters (Stephanie, Alexa, and Tory) for their support.

Kevin Auman and Donna Campbell, partners in this project.

Kerry Bruce, for her valuable assistance; Celia Miles for proofreading; and Abby Auman for help with photos.

Richard Cornelius and Allan Fisher, for inspiration and lessons I hope I've learned.

The Juntas (Ray, John, Brooks, and Fred), The Inkblots (Sallie, Kathleen, Laurel, Charlie, and Robert), and all those who attend the Writer's Coffee at Barnes and Noble, Wednesdays at 3 P.M., in Asheville, North Carolina. Asheville is an amazing, supportive writers' community.

Last but not least, thank you, Lorraine. Only you know how much I owe you.

—Stephen Griffith

SOURCES

Jim Bakker, Barbara Bush, Patricia Cornwell, Leighton Ford, Gay Currie Fox, Jean Graham Ford, Billy Graham, Franklin Graham, Dr. Olson Huff, Jan Karon, Anne Graham Lotz, Andie McDowell, Rosa Bell Montgomery, Kitty Peterson, Claudia (Ladybird) Johnson, George Beverly Shea, Karlene Shea, Gigi Graham Tchividjian, Calvin Thielmann, and Richard Jesse Watson. Interviews by Donna Campbell, Stephen Griffith, and others for the television special "Ruth and Billy Graham: What Grace Provides." UNC-TV, Jan. 14, 2002. Used by permission of Donna Campbell, producer.

Barker, Berdjette, Evelyn Freeland, and Mauric Scobie. Interviews by Stephen Griffith and Kevin Auman recorded in Spring 2003. Used by permission of Stone Table Media.

Eisenhower, Julie Nixon. *Special People.* New York: Simon & Schuster, 1977. Copyright © 1977. Used by permission.

Frist, Betty. *My Neighbors, the Billy Grahams.* Nashville: Broadman Press, 1983. Used by permission.

Graham, Billy. *Just As I Am.* New York: HarperCollins Worldwide, 1997. Copyright © 1997 by the Billy Graham Evangelistic Association. Excerpts reprinted by permission of HarperCollins Publishers, Inc.

Graham, Franklin. *Rebel with a Cause.* Nashville: Thomas Nelson, 1995. Reprinted by permission of Thomas Nelson Publishers from *Rebel with a* Cause, copyright 1995 by Franklin Graham.

Graham, Ruth Bell. "As the Portrait Is Unconscious," "Sitting by My Laughing Fire," "I'm Daniel Creasman's Mother," "Give Me a Cove," and "And When I Die." *Collected Poems.* Grand Rapids, Mich.: Baker Book House, 1977, 1992, 1997, 1998. Used by permission of Baker Book House.

Graham, Ruth Bell. Interview by Wesley Pippert. First appeared in *Christian Life Magazine*, May 1972. Used by Permission.

Kawasaki, Guy. *Hindsights: The Wisdom and Breakthroughs of Remarkable People.* Copyright © 1993 by Guy Kawasaki, Beyond Words Publishing, Inc., Hillsboro, Oregon, USA.

McIntyre, Ruth Graham. Original material used by permission of Ruth Graham McIntyre.

Pollock, John. *A Foreign Devil in China.* Minneapolis: World Wide Publications, 1971, 1988. Used by permission of Ruth Bell Graham.

Seera, Betty Ruth. Original material used by permission.

Tchividjian, Gigi Graham. Quoted in Ruth Bell Graham. *Footprints of a Pilgrim.* Nashville: Word Publishing, 2001. Used by permission.

Tripp, Rhoda Thomas, comp. *The International Thesaurus of Quotations.* New York: Harper & Row Publishers, 1970.